Concise Rules of
APA Style

Sixth Edition

Concise Rules of
APA Style

American Psychological Association • *Washington, DC*

Second printing: September 2009
Third printing: October 2009
Fourth printing: June 2010

Published by
American Psychological Association
750 First Street, NE
Washington, DC 20002
www.apa.org

To order
APA Order Department
P.O. Box 92984
Washington, DC 20090-2984
Tel: (800) 374-2721; Direct: (202) 336-5510
Fax: (202) 336-5502; TDD/TTY: (202) 336-6123
Online: www.apa.org/books/
E-mail: order@apa.org

In the U.K., Europe, Africa, and the Middle East, copies may be ordered from
American Psychological Association
3 Henrietta Street
Covent Garden, London
WC2E 8LU England

Typeset in Sabon and Univers by Circle Graphics, Columbia, MD
Printer: United Book Press, Baltimore, MD
Cover Designer: Naylor Design, Washington, DC
Production Manager: Jennifer L. Macomber
Editorial Director: Mary Lynn Skutley
Senior Editor, APA Style: Anne W. Gasque

Library of Congress Cataloging-in-Publication Data

Concise rules of APA style. — 6th ed.
       p. cm.
   Includes bibliographical references and index.
   ISBN-13: 978-1-4338-0560-8 (spiral bound)
   ISBN-10: 1-4338-0560-X (spiral bound)
   1. Psychology—Authorship—Style manuals. 2. Social sciences—Authorship—Handbooks, manuals, etc. I. American Psychological Association.

   BF76.7.C66 2010
   808'.06615—dc22

                                                                 2009011709

British Library Cataloguing-in-Publication Data
A CIP record is available from the British Library.

Printed in the United States of America
Sixth Edition

Contents

3. Italicizing and Abbreviating   *73*

4. Numbers, Metrication, and Statistics   *85*

Concise Rules of
APA Style

Introduction: A Pocket Reference for Writers

oncise Rules of APA Style was first published in 2005 as the official pocket style guide from the American Psychological Association. Drawn from the sixth edition of the *Publication Manual of the American Psychological Association* (2010), this edition of *Concise Rules* focuses on what generally comes to mind when we talk about style—the rules that govern scientific communication: Which numbers are expressed as numerals? Which words are capitalized? How do I structure a footnote? Create a table? Credit my sources? Structure a reference list?

The *Publication Manual* is a complete guide to the full enterprise of scientific writing. It covers everything from the ethics of determining authorship to journal article reporting standards to the nature of the peer review process. In contrast, *Concise Rules* contains just the nuts-and-bolts rules that writers need at their fingertips as they work.

Organization

In Chapter 1, we offer basic guidance on planning and writing an article. We advise readers on how to organize their thoughts, choose effective words, and describe individuals with accuracy and sensitivity.

In Chapter 2, we describe the style for APA journals regarding punctuation, spelling, and capitalization.

In Chapter 3, we provide guidelines on the use of italics and abbreviations in scientific writing.

In Chapter 4, we describe the style for presenting numbers, metrication, and statistics in scientific writing. The sections within this chapter present rules, exceptions, and special usages of numbers; recommendations on using the metric system in journals; and guidelines on presenting statistical and mathematical copy.

In Chapter 5, we describe the effective use of graphic elements in text and provide readers with illustrations of graphic elements that are useful for the presentation of data in tables and figures.

In Chapter 6, we describe how footnotes, appendices, and supplemental material can be used to present material that is nonessential to the main text.

In Chapter 7, we provide guidance on citing sources. We discuss ground rules for acknowledging the contributions of others and for formatting quotations. We instruct readers on when and how to cite references in text and on how to construct a reference list that contains everything readers need to locate each source.

In Chapter 8, we provide a comprehensive selection of reference examples in APA Style. The examples cover a range of categories, from periodicals to podcasts, with an emphasis on references to electronic formats.

New in This Edition

In Chapter 1, we offer two areas with significantly changed content. First, we have simplified APA heading style to make it more conducive to electronic publication. Second, we have updated guidelines for reducing bias in language to reflect current practices and preferences. A new section on presenting historical language that is inappropriate by present standards has been added, and examples of good and bad language choices have been expanded and moved to the web, where they are more accessible to all and can be easily updated.

New content in Chapter 4 includes guidelines for reporting inferential statistics and a significantly revised table of statistical abbreviations.

Chapter 5 contains significantly expanded content on the electronic presentation of data. It will help readers understand the purpose of each kind of display and choose the best match for communicating the results of the investigation. The chapter provides new examples for a variety of displays, including electrophysiological, imaging, and other biological data.

Chapter 6 provides new guidelines on the use of supplemental material to be place in online supplemental archives.

In Chapter 7, the discussion of electronic sources has been greatly expanded, emphasizing the role of the digital object identifier as a reliable way to locate information. The discussion of each reference type is now followed directly by a variety of examples, with electronic sources featured.

Chapter 8 contains a significantly expanded set of reference examples, with an emphasis on electronic formats, for readers to use in mastering the changes described in Chapter 7. New examples have been added for a number of online sources, from data sets and measurement instruments to software and online discussion forums.

We encourage readers to supplement the information in this book by consulting the APA Style website (www.apastyle.org), which offers invaluable information and resources on a variety of topics as well as style tips, frequently asked questions, and resources for new writers. Our hope is that the style tools we offer will simplify your life, strengthen your writing, and improve the caliber of scholarly communications.

1

Concise and Bias-Free Writing

This chapter provides some general principles of expository writing and suggests ways to improve writing style. We focus first on the benefits of planning and choosing the best organizational structure to develop your argument. We next describe some basic principles for writing with clarity and precision and for avoiding bias in language. Last, we demonstrate how correct grammar is the foundation of clear, effective, and persuasive communication.

Organization

Before beginning to write, consider the best length and structure for the findings you wish to share. Ordering your thoughts logically, both at the paragraph and at the sentence levels, will strengthen the impact of your writing.

1.01 Length

The optimal length of a manuscript is the number of pages needed to effectively communicate the primary ideas of the study, review, or theoretical analysis. As a rule, "less is more." Discursive writing often obscures an author's main points, and condensing long manuscripts often improves them. If a paper is too long, shorten it by stating points clearly and directly, confining the discussion to the specific problem under investigation, deleting or combining data displays, eliminating repetition across sections, and writing in the active voice. At times, a paper may need to be divided into two or more papers, each with a more specific focus (for guidance on avoiding the ethical risk of duplicate or piecemeal publication, see the *Publication Manual of the American Psychological Association* [*Publication Manual*], 2010, section 1.09). Journals differ in average length of articles published. Strive to be consistent with the practices of the journal to which you are submitting your paper.

1.02 Organizing a Manuscript With Headings

In scientific writing, sound organizational structure is the key to clear, precise, and logical communication. This includes the use of headings to effectively organize ideas within a study as well as seriation to highlight important items within sections. Concise headings help the reader anticipate key points and track the development of your argument.

Readers familiar with previous rules of APA Style will note that we have changed and simplified the heading styles in this edition. This change was motivated by the desire to make planning a less complicated process for the writer and to make articles more accessible for those reading them in electronic formats.

Levels of heading establish the hierarchy of sections via format or appearance. All topics of equal importance have the same level of heading throughout a manuscript. For example, in a multiexperiment paper, the headings for the Method and Results sections in Experiment 1 should be the same level as the headings for the Method and Results sections in Experiment 2.

Avoid having only one subsection heading and subsection within a section, just as you would in an outline. Use at least two subsection headings within any given section, or use none (e.g., in an outline, you could divide a section numbered I into a minimum of A and B sections; just an A section could not stand alone).

1.03 Levels of Heading

The heading style recommended by APA consists of five possible formatting arrangements, according to the number of levels of subordination. Each heading level is numbered (see Table 1.1).

Regardless of the number of levels of subheading within a section, the heading structure for all sections follows the same top-down progression. Each section starts with the highest level of heading, even if one section may have fewer levels of subheading than another section. For example, the Method and Results sections of a paper

Table 1.1. Format for Five Levels of Heading in APA Journals

Level of heading	Format
1	Centered, Boldface, Uppercase and Lowercase Heading[a]
2	Flush Left, Boldface, Uppercase and Lowercase Heading
3	Indented, boldface, lowercase paragraph heading ending with a period.[b]
4	*Indented, boldface, italicized, lowercase paragraph heading ending with a period.*
5	*Indented, italicized, lowercase paragraph heading ending with a period.*

[a]This type of capitalization is also referred to as *title case*. [b]In a *lowercase paragraph heading,* the first letter of the first word is uppercase and the remaining words are lowercase.

may each have two levels of subheading, and the Discussion section may have only one level of subheading. There would then be three levels of heading for the paper overall: the section headings (**Method, Results,** and **Discussion**) and the two levels of subheading, as follows:

Method

Sample and Participant Selection

Assessments and Measures

> **Q-sort measures of inhibition and aggressiveness.**

> **Life History Calendar.**

Results

Outcome of Inhibited Children at 23 Years

> **Personality and self-esteem.**

> **Social network.**

> **Life history and IQ.**

Outcome of Aggressive Children at 23 Years

Discussion

Inhibited Children: Delayed Social Transitions During Emerging Adulthood

Inhibited Children: Weak Evidence for Internalizing Difficulties

Limitations of the Present Study

Conclusions and Future Prospects

The introduction to a manuscript does not carry a heading that labels it as the introduction. (The first part of a manuscript is assumed to be the introduction.)

Do not label headings with numbers or letters. (The sections and headings in *Concise Rules of APA Style* are numbered only to permit indexing and cross-referencing.) The number of levels of heading needed for your article will depend on its length and complexity. If only one level of heading is needed, use Level 1; for a paper with two levels of heading, use Levels 1 and 2; if three levels are needed, use Levels 1, 2, and 3; and so forth.

1.04 Seriation

Just as the heading structure alerts readers to the order of ideas within the paper, seriation helps the reader understand the organization of key points within sections, paragraphs, and sentences. In any series, all items should be syntactically and conceptually parallel (see section 1.23).

Separate paragraphs in a series, such as itemized conclusions or steps in a procedure, are identified by an Arabic numeral followed by a period but not enclosed in or followed by parentheses. Separate sentences in a series are also identified by an Arabic numeral followed by a period; the first word is capitalized, and the sentence ends with a period or correct punctuation.

> Using the learned helplessness theory, we predicted that the depressed and nondepressed participants would make the following judgments of control:
>
> 1. Individuals who . . . [paragraph continues].
>
> 2. Nondepressed persons exposed to . . . [paragraph continues].
>
> 3. Depressed persons exposed to . . . [paragraph continues].
>
> 4. Depressed and nondepressed participants in the no-noise groups . . . [paragraph continues].

The use of "numbered lists" may connote an unwanted or unwarranted ordinal position (e.g., chronology, importance, priority) among the items. If you wish to achieve the same effect without the implication of ordinality, items in the series should be identified by bullets. Symbols such as small squares, circles, and so forth, may be used in creating a bulleted list. At the time that an article accepted for publication is typeset, the bullet notation will be changed to the style used by that journal.

- Individuals who . . . [paragraph continues].

- Nondepressed persons exposed to . . . [paragraph continues].

- Depressed persons exposed to . . . [paragraph continues].

- Depressed and nondepressed participants in the no-noise groups . . . [paragraph continues].

Within a paragraph or sentence, identify elements in a series by lowercase letters in parentheses.

> The participant's three choices were (a) working with another participant, (b) working with a team, and (c) working alone.

Within a sentence, use commas to separate three or more elements that do not have internal commas; use semicolons to separate three or more elements that have internal commas.

> We tested three groups: (a) low scorers, who scored fewer than 20 points; (b) moderate scorers, who scored between 20 and 50 points; and (c) high scorers, who scored more than 50 points.

Alternatively, you may use bulleted lists within a sentence to separate three or more elements. In these instances, capitalize and punctuate the list as if it were a complete sentence.

> In accordance with this theory, these relations should be marked by
>
> - equity, social justice, and equal opportunity;
>
> - sensitivity to individual differences and promotion of a goodness-of-fit between individually different people and contexts;
>
> - affirmative actions to correct ontogenetic or historical inequities in person–context fit;

- efforts to recognize and celebrate diversity; and

- promotion of universal participation in civic life, and hence democracy (Lerner, Balsano, Banik, & Naudeau, 2005, p. 45).

Writing Style

The prime objective of scientific reporting is clear communication. You can achieve this by presenting ideas in an orderly manner and by expressing yourself smoothly and precisely. Establishing a tone that conveys the essential points of your study in an interesting manner will engage readers and communicate your ideas more effectively.

1.05 Continuity in Presentation of Ideas

Readers will better understand your ideas if you aim for continuity in words, concepts, and thematic development from the opening statement to the conclusion. Continuity can be achieved in several ways. For instance, punctuation marks contribute to continuity by showing relationships between ideas. They cue the reader to the pauses, inflections, subordination, and pacing normally heard in speech. Use the full range of punctuation aids available: Neither overuse nor underuse one type of punctuation, such as commas or dashes. Overuse may annoy the reader; underuse may confuse. Instead, use punctuation to support meaning.

Another way to achieve continuity is through the use of transitional words. These words help maintain the flow of thought, especially when the material is complex or abstract. A pronoun that refers to a noun in the preceding sentence not only serves as a transition but also avoids repetition. Be sure the referent is obvious. Other transition devices are time links (*then, next, after, while, since*), cause–effect links (*therefore, consequently, as a result*), addition links (*in addition, moreover, furthermore, similarly*), and contrast links (*but, conversely, nevertheless, however, although*).

1.06 Smoothness of Expression

Scientific prose and creative writing serve different purposes. Devices that are often found in creative writing—for example, setting up ambiguity; inserting the unexpected; omitting the expected; and suddenly shifting the topic, tense, or person—can confuse or disturb readers of scientific prose. Therefore, try to avoid these devices and aim for clear and logical communication.

Because you have been so close to your material, you may not immediately see certain problems, especially contradictions the reader may infer. A reading by a colleague may uncover such problems. You can usually catch omissions, irrelevancies, and abruptness by putting the manuscript aside and rereading it later. Reading the paper aloud can make flaws more apparent. (See also section 1.11.)

If, on later reading, you find that your writing is abrupt, introducing more transition devices may be helpful. You may have abandoned an argument or theme prematurely; if so, you need to amplify the discussion.

Abruptness may result from sudden, unnecessary shifts in verb tense within the same paragraph or in adjacent paragraphs. By using verb tenses consistently, you can help ensure smooth expression. Past tense (e.g., "Smith *showed*") or present perfect tense (e.g., "researchers *have shown*") is appropriate for the literature review and the description of the procedure if the discussion is of past events. Stay within the chosen tense. Use past tense (e.g., "anxiety *decreased* significantly") to describe the results. Use the present tense (e.g., "the results of Experiment 2 *indicate*") to discuss implications of the results and to present the conclusions. By reporting conclusions in the present tense, you allow readers to join you in deliberating the matter at hand. (See section 1.18 for details on the use of verb tense.)

Noun strings, meaning several nouns used one after another to modify a final noun, create another form of abruptness. The reader is sometimes forced to stop to determine how the words relate to one another. Skillful hyphenation can clarify the relationships between words, but often the best approach is to untangle the string. For example, consider the following string:

> commonly used investigative expanded issue control question technique

This is dense prose to the reader knowledgeable about studies on lie detection—and gibberish to a reader unfamiliar with such studies. Possible ways to untangle the string are as follows:

- a control-question technique that is commonly used to expand issues in investigations

- an expanded-issue control-question technique that is commonly used in investigations

- a common technique of using control questions to investigate expanded issues

- a common investigative technique of using expanded issues in control questions

One approach to untangling noun strings is to move the last word to the beginning of the string and fill in with verbs and prepositions. For example, *early childhood thought disorder misdiagnosis* might be rearranged to read *misdiagnosis of thought disorders in early childhood*.

Many writers strive to achieve smooth expression by using synonyms or near-synonyms to avoid repeating a term. The intention is commendable, but by using synonyms you may unintentionally suggest a subtle difference. Therefore, choose synonyms with care. The discreet use of pronouns can often relieve the monotonous repetition of a term without introducing ambiguity.

1.07 Tone

Although scientific writing differs in form from literary writing, it need not lack style or be dull. In describing your research, present the ideas and findings directly but aim for an interesting and compelling style and a tone that reflects your involvement with the problem.

Scientific writing often contrasts the positions of different researchers. Differences should be presented in a professional, noncombative manner. For example, "Fong and Nisbett did not address . . ." is acceptable, whereas "Fong and Nisbett completely overlooked . . ." is not.

One effective way to achieve the right tone is to imagine a specific reader you are intending to reach and to write in a way that will educate and persuade that individual. Envisioning a person familiar to you may make this technique more effective. You may wish to write, for example, to a researcher in a related field who is trying to keep abreast of the literature but is not familiar with jargon or insider perspectives. What would facilitate his or her understanding of and appreciation for the importance of your work?

1.08 Economy of Expression

Say only what needs to be said. The author who is frugal with words not only writes a more readable manuscript but also increases the chances that the manuscript will be accepted for publication. The number of printed pages a journal can publish is limited, and editors therefore often request that authors shorten submitted papers. You can tighten long papers by eliminating redundancy, wordiness, jargon, evasiveness, overuse of the passive voice, circumlocution, and clumsy prose. Weed out overly detailed descriptions of apparatus, participants, or procedures (for guidance, see APA Publications and Communications Board Working Group on Journal Article Reporting Standards, 2008, or Chapter 2 in the *Publication Manual*, APA, 2010); elaborations of the obvious; and irrelevant observations or asides. Materials such as these may be placed, when appropriate, in an online supplemental archive (see section 6.04 for further details).

Short words and short sentences are easier to comprehend than are long ones. A long technical term, however, may be more precise than several short words, and technical terms are inseparable from scientific reporting.

Yet the technical terminology in a paper should be readily understood by individuals throughout each discipline. An article that depends on terminology familiar to only a few specialists does not sufficiently contribute to the literature.

Wordiness. Wordiness can also impede the ready grasp of ideas. Change *based on the fact that* to *because, at the present time* to *now*, and *for the purpose of* to simply *for* or *to*. Use *this study* instead of *the present study* when the context is clear. Change *there were several students who completed* to *several students completed*. Unconstrained wordiness lapses into embellishment and flowery writing, which are clearly inappropriate in scientific style.

Redundancy. Writers often use redundant language in an effort to be emphatic. Use no more words than are necessary to convey your meaning.

In the following examples, the italicized words are redundant and should be omitted:

they were *both* alike	*one and* the same
a total of 68 participants	in *close* proximity
four *different* groups saw	*completely* unanimous
instructions, which were *exactly* the same as those used	*just* exactly
	very close to significance
absolutely essential	*period of* time
has been *previously* found	summarize *briefly*
small *in size*	the reason is *because*

Unit length. Although writing only in short, simple sentences produces choppy and boring prose, writing exclusively in long, involved sentences results in difficult, sometimes incomprehensible material. Varied sentence length helps readers maintain interest and comprehension. When involved concepts require long sentences, the components should proceed logically. Direct, declarative sentences with simple, common words are usually best.

Similar cautions apply to paragraph length. Single-sentence paragraphs are abrupt. Paragraphs that are too long are likely to lose the reader's attention. A new paragraph provides a pause for the reader—a chance to assimilate one step in the conceptual development before beginning another. If a paragraph runs longer than one double-spaced manuscript page, you may lose your readers. Look for a logical place to break a long paragraph or reorganize the material.

1.09 Precision and Clarity

Word choice. Make certain that every word means exactly what you intend it to mean. In informal style, for example, *feel* broadly substitutes for *think* or *believe*, but in scientific style such latitude is not acceptable. A similar example is that *like* is often used when *such as* is meant:

> *Correct:*
>
> Articles by psychologists such as Skinner and Watson. . . .
>
> *Correct:*
>
> Like Watson, Skinner believed. . . .
>
> *Incorrect:*
>
> Articles by psychologists like Skinner and Watson. . . .

Colloquial expressions. Avoid colloquial expressions (e.g., *write up* for *report*), which diffuse meaning. Approximations of quantity (e.g., *quite a large part, practically all*, or *very few*) are interpreted differently by different readers or in different contexts. Approximations weaken statements, especially those describing empirical observations.

Jargon. *Jargon* is the continuous use of a technical vocabulary, even in places where that vocabulary is not relevant. Jargon is also the substitution of a euphemistic phrase for a familiar term (e.g., *monetarily felt scarcity* for *poverty*), and you should scrupulously avoid using such jargon. Federal bureaucratic jargon has had the greatest publicity, but scientific jargon also grates on the reader, encumbers the communication of information, and wastes space.

Pronouns. Pronouns confuse readers unless the referent for each pronoun is obvious; readers should not have to search previous text to determine the meaning of the term. Pronouns such as *this, that, these,* and *those* can be troublesome when they refer to something or someone in a previous sentence. Eliminate ambiguity by writing, for example, *this test, that trial, these participants,* and *those reports* (see also section 1.20).

Comparisons. Ambiguous or illogical comparisons result from omission of key verbs or from nonparallel structure. Consider, for example, "Ten-year-olds were more likely to play with age peers than 8-year-olds." Does this sentence mean that 10-year-olds were more likely than 8-year-olds to play with age peers? Or does it mean that 10-year-olds were more likely to play with age peers and less likely to play with 8-year-olds? An illogical comparison occurs when parallelism is overlooked for the sake of brevity, as in "Her salary was lower than a convenience store clerk." Thoughtful attention to good sentence structure and word choice reduces the chance of this kind of ambiguity.

Attribution. Inappropriately or illogically attributing action in an effort to be objective can be misleading. Examples of undesirable attribution include use of the third person, anthropomorphism, and use of the editorial *we*.

Third person. To avoid ambiguity, use a personal pronoun rather than the third person when describing steps taken in your experiment.

Correct:

We reviewed the literature.

Incorrect:

> The authors reviewed the literature.

Anthropomorphism. Do not attribute human characteristics to animals or to inanimate sources.

Correct:

> Pairs of rats (cage mates) were allowed to forage together.

Incorrect:

> Rat couples (cage mates) were allowed to forage together.

Correct:

> The staff for the community program was persuaded to allow five of the observers to become tutors.

Incorrect:

> The community program was persuaded to allow five of the observers to become tutors.

An experiment cannot *attempt to demonstrate, control unwanted variables*, or *interpret findings*, nor can tables or figures *compare* (all of these can, however, *show* or *indicate*). Use a pronoun or an appropriate noun as the subject of these verbs. *I* or *we* (meaning the author or authors) can replace *the experiment*.

Editorial we. For clarity, restrict your use of *we* to refer only to yourself and your coauthors (use *I* if you are the sole author of the paper). Broader uses of *we* may leave your readers wondering to whom you are referring; instead, substitute an appropriate noun or clarify your usage:

Correct:

> Researchers usually classify birdsong on the basis of frequency and temporal structure of the elements.

Incorrect:

> We usually classify birdsong on the basis of frequency and temporal structure of the elements.

Some alternatives to *we* to consider are *people*, *humans*, *researchers*, *psychologists*, *nurses*, and so on. *We* is an appropriate and useful referent:

Correct:

> As behaviorists, we tend to dispute . . .

Incorrect:

> We tend to dispute . . .

1.10   Linguistic Devices

Devices that attract attention to words, sounds, or other embellishments instead of to ideas are inappropriate in scientific writing. Avoid heavy alliteration, rhyming, poetic expressions, and clichés. Use metaphors sparingly; although they can help simplify complicated ideas, metaphors can be distracting. Avoid mixed metaphors (e.g., *a theory representing one branch of a growing body of evidence*) and words with surplus or unintended meaning (e.g., *cop* for *police officer*), which may distract if not actually mislead the reader. Use figurative expressions with restraint and colorful expressions with care; these expressions can sound strained or forced.

1.11   Strategies to Improve Writing Style

Authors use various strategies in putting their thoughts on paper. The fit between author and strategy is more important than the particular strategy used. Three approaches to achieving professional and effective communication are (a) writing from an outline; (b) putting aside the first draft, then rereading it later; and (c) asking a colleague to review and critique the draft for you.

Writing from an outline helps preserve the logic of the research itself. An outline identifies main ideas, defines subordinate ideas, helps you discipline your writing and avoid tangential excursions, and helps you notice omissions. In an outline, you can also identify the sub-headings that will be used in the article itself.

Rereading your own copy after setting it aside for a few days permits a fresh approach. Reading the paper aloud enables you not only to see faults that you over-looked on the previous reading but also to hear them. When these problems are corrected, give a polished copy to a colleague—preferably a person who has published in a related field but who is not familiar with your own work—for a critical review. Even better, get critiques from two colleagues, and you will have a trial run of a journal's review process.

These strategies, particularly the latter, may require you to invest more time in a manuscript than you had an-ticipated. The results of these strategies, however, may be greater accuracy and thoroughness and clearer commu-nication.

Reducing Bias in Language

Scientific writing must be free of implied or irrelevant evaluation of the group or groups being studied. As an organization, APA is committed both to science and to the fair treatment of individuals and groups, and this pol-icy requires that authors who write for APA publications avoid perpetuating demeaning attitudes and biased as-sumptions about people in their writing. Constructions that might imply bias against persons on the basis of gen-der, sexual orientation, racial or ethnic group, disability, or age are unacceptable.

Long-standing cultural practice can exert a powerful influence over even the most conscientious author. Just as you have learned to check what you write for spelling, grammar, and wordiness, practice rereading your work for bias. Another suggestion is to ask people from targeted groups to read and comment on your material.

What follows is a set of guidelines and discussions of specific issues that affect particular groups. These are not rigid rules. You may find that some attempts to follow the guidelines result in wordiness or clumsy prose. As always, good judgment is required. If your writing reflects respect for your participants and your readers and if you write with appropriate specificity and precision, you will be contributing to the goal of accurate, unbiased communication. Specific examples for each guideline are given in the Guidelines for Unbiased Language, which can be found on the APA Style website (www.apastyle.org).

General Guidelines for Reducing Bias

Guideline 1: Describe at the Appropriate Level of Specificity

Precision is essential in scientific writing; when you refer to a person or persons, choose words that are accurate, clear, and free from bias. The appropriate degree of specificity depends on the research question and the present state of knowledge in the field of study. When in doubt, be more specific rather than less because it is easier to aggregate published data than to disaggregate them. For example, using *man* to refer to all human beings is simply not as accurate as the phrase *women and men*. To describe age groups, give a specific age range ("ages 65–83 years") instead of a broad category ("over 65 years"; see Schaie, 1993). When describing racial and ethnic groups, be appropriately specific and sensitive to issues of labeling. For example, instead of describing participants as Asian American or Hispanic American, it may be helpful to describe them by their nation or region of origin (e.g., Chinese Americans, Mexican Americans). If you are discussing sexual orientation, realize that some people interpret *gay* as referring to men and women, whereas others interpret the term as referring only to men (the terms *gay men* and *lesbians* currently are preferred).

Broad clinical terms such as *borderline* and *at risk* are loaded with innuendo unless properly explained. Specify the diagnosis that is borderline (e.g., "people with borderline personality disorder"). Identify the risk and the people it involves (e.g., "children at risk for early school dropout").

Gender is cultural and is the term to use when referring to women and men as social groups. *Sex* is biological; use it when the biological distinction is predominant. Note that the word *sex* can be confused with *sexual behavior*. *Gender* helps keep meaning unambiguous, as in the following example: "In accounting for attitudes toward the bill, sexual orientation rather than gender accounted for most of the variance. Most gay men and lesbians were for the proposal; most heterosexual men and women were against it."

Part of writing without bias is recognizing that differences should be mentioned only when relevant. Marital status, sexual orientation, racial and ethnic identity, or the fact that a person has a disability should not be mentioned gratuitously.

Guideline 2: Be Sensitive to Labels

Respect people's preferences; call people what they prefer to be called. Accept that preferences change with time and that individuals within groups often disagree about the designations they prefer. Make an effort to determine what is appropriate for your situation; you may need to ask your participants which designations they prefer, particularly when preferred designations are being debated within groups.

Avoid labeling people when possible. A common occurrence in scientific writing is that participants in a study tend to lose their individuality; they are broadly categorized as objects (noun forms such as *the gays* and *the elderly*) or, particularly in descriptions of people with disabilities, are equated with their conditions—*the amnesiacs*, *the depressives*, *the schizophrenics*, *the LDs*, for example. One solution is to use adjectival forms (e.g., "gay *men*," "older *adults*," "amnesic *patients*"). Another is to "put the person first," followed by a descriptive phrase (e.g., "people diagnosed with schizophrenia"). Note that the latter solution currently is preferred when describing people with disabilities.

When you need to mention several groups in a sentence or paragraph, such as when reporting results, do your best to balance sensitivity, clarity, and parsimony. For example, it may be cumbersome to repeat phrases such as "person with _____." If you provide operational definitions of groups early in your paper (e.g., "Participants scoring a minimum of X on the X scale constituted the high verbal group, and those scoring below X constituted the low verbal group"), it is scientifically informative and concise to describe participants thereafter in terms of the measures used to classify them (e.g., ". . . the contrast for the high verbal group was statistically significant, $p = .043$"), provided the terms are inoffensive. A label should not be used in any form that is perceived as pejorative; if such a perception is possible, you need to find more neutral terms. For example, *the demented* is not repaired by changing it to *demented group*, but *dementia group* would be acceptable. Abbreviations or series labels for groups usually sacrifice clarity and may offend: *LDs* or *LD group* to describe people with specific learning difficulties is offensive; *HVAs* for "high verbal ability group" is difficult to decipher. *Group A* is not offensive, but it is not descriptive either.

Recognize the difference between *case*, which is an occurrence of a disorder or illness, and *patient*, which is a person affected by the disorder or illness and receiving a doctor's care. "Manic–depressive cases were treated" is problematic; revise to "The patients with bipolar disorders were treated."

Bias may be promoted when the writer uses one group (often the writer's own group) as the standard against which others are judged, for example, citizens of the United States. In some contexts, the term *culturally deprived* may imply that one culture is the universally accepted standard. The unparallel nouns in the phrase *man and wife* may inappropriately prompt the reader to evaluate the roles of the individuals (i.e., the woman is defined only in terms of her relationship to the man) and the motives of the author. By contrast, the phrases *husband and wife* and *man and woman* are parallel. Usage of *normal* may prompt the reader to make the comparison with *abnormal,* thus stigmatizing individuals with differences. For example, contrasting lesbians with "the general public" or with "normal women" portrays lesbians as marginal to society. More appropriate comparison groups might be *heterosexual women, heterosexual women and men,* or *gay men.*

Also be aware of how order of presentation of social groups can imply that the first-mentioned group is the norm or standard and that later mentioned groups are deviant. Thus the phrases *men and women* and *White Americans and racial minorities* subtly reflect the perceived dominance of men and Whites over other groups. Similarly, when presenting group data, consider how placing socially dominant groups such as men and Whites on the left side of graphs and/or top of tables may also imply that these groups are the universal standard (Hegarty & Buechel, 2006). Avoid a consistent pattern of presenting information about socially dominant groups first.

Guideline 3: Acknowledge Participation

Write about the people in your study in a way that acknowledges their participation but is also consistent with the traditions of the field in which you are working. Thus, although descriptive terms such as *college students, children,* or *respondents* provide precise information about the individuals taking part in a research project, the more general terms *participants* and *subjects* are also in common usage. Indeed, for more than 100 years the term *subjects* has been used within experimental psychology as a general starting point for describing a sample, and its use is appropriate. *Subjects* and *sample* are customary when discussing certain established statistical terms (e.g., *within-subject* and *between-subjects* design). Further, the passive voice suggests individuals are *acted on* instead of being actors ("the students *completed* the survey" is preferable to "the students *were given* the survey" or "the survey was *administered* to the students"). "The subjects *completed* the trial" or "we *collected* data from the participants" is preferable to "the participants *were run*." Consider avoiding terms such as *patient management* and *patient placement* when appropriate. In most cases, it is the treatment, not patients, that is managed; some alternatives are *coordination of care*, *supportive services*, and *assistance*. Also avoid the term *failed*, as in "eight participants failed to complete the Rorschach and the MMPI," because it can imply a personal shortcoming instead of a research result; *did not* is a more neutral choice (Knatterud, 1991).

As you read the rest of this chapter, consult the www.apastyle.org for specific examples of problematic and preferred language in the Guidelines for Unbiased Language as well as further resources and information about nondiscriminatory language.

Reducing Bias by Topic

1.12 Gender

Remember that *gender* refers to role, not biological sex, and is cultural. Avoid ambiguity in sex identity or gender role by choosing nouns, pronouns, and adjectives that specifically describe your participants. Sexist bias can occur when pronouns are used carelessly, as when the masculine pronoun *he* is used to refer to both sexes or when the masculine or feminine pronoun is used exclusively to define roles by sex (e.g., "the nurse . . . *she*"). The use of *man* as a generic noun or as an ending for an occupational title (e.g., *policeman* instead of *police officer*) can be ambiguous and may imply incorrectly that all persons in the group are male. Be clear about whether you mean one sex or both sexes.

There are many alternatives to the generic *he* (see the Guidelines for Unbiased Language at www.apastyle.org), including rephrasing (e.g., from "When an individual conducts this kind of self-appraisal, *he* is a much stronger person" to "When an individual conducts this kind of self-appraisal, that person is much stronger" or "This kind of self-appraisal makes an individual much stronger"), using plural nouns or plural pronouns (e.g., from "A therapist who is too much like his client can lose *his* objectivity" to "Therapists who are too much like their clients can lose *their* objectivity"), replacing the pronoun with an article (e.g., from "A researcher must apply for *his* grant by September 1" to "A researcher must apply for *the* grant by September 1"), and dropping the pronoun (e.g., from "The researcher must avoid letting *his* own biases and expectations influence the interpretation of the results" to "The researcher must avoid letting biases and expectations influence the interpretation of the results"). Replacing *he* with *he or she* or *she or he* should be done sparingly because the repetition can become tiresome. Combination forms such as *he/she* or *(s)he* are awkward and distracting. Alternating between *he* and *she* also may be distracting and is not ideal; doing so implies that *he* or *she* can in fact be generic, which is not the case. Use of either pronoun unavoidably suggests that specific gender to the reader. Avoid referring to one sex as the *opposite sex*: an appropriate wording is the *other sex*. The term *opposite sex* implies strong differences between the two sexes; however, in fact, there are more similarities than differences between the two sexes (e.g., Hyde, 2005).

The adjective *transgender* refers to persons whose gender identity or gender expression differs from their sex at birth; *transgender* should not be used as a noun (National Lesbian & Gay Journalists Association, 2005). The word *transsexual* refers to transgender persons who live or desire to live full time as members of the sex other than their sex at birth, many of whom wish to make their bodies as congruent as possible with their preferred sex through surgery and hormonal treatment (American Psychiatric Association, 2000; Meyer et al., 2001). *Transsexual* can be used as a noun or as an adjective. The terms *female-to-male transgender person*, *male-to-female transgender person*, *female-to-male transsexual*, and *male-to-female transsexual* represent accepted usage (Gay & Lesbian Alliance Against Defamation, 2007). Transsexuals undergo *sex reassignment*, a term that is preferable to *sex change*. *Cross-dresser* is preferable to *transvestite*.

Refer to a transgender person using words (proper nouns, pronouns, etc.) appropriate to the person's gender identity or gender expression, regardless of birth sex. For example, use the pronouns *he*, *him*, or *his* in reference to a female-to-male transgender person. If gender identity or gender expression is ambiguous or variable, it may be best to avoid pronouns, as discussed earlier in this section (for more detailed information, see www.apastyle.org).

1.13 Sexual Orientation

Sexual orientation refers to an enduring pattern of attraction, behavior, emotion, identity, and social contacts. The term *sexual orientation* should be used rather than *sexual preference*. For a person having a bisexual orientation, the orientation is not chosen even though the sex of the partner may be a choice. For more information, see *Guidelines for Psychotherapy With Lesbian, Gay, and Bisexual Clients* (APA Committee on Lesbian, Gay, and Bisexual Concerns Joint Task Force on Guidelines for Psychotherapy With Lesbian, Gay, and Bisexual Clients, 2000; see also www.apastyle.org).

The terms *lesbians*, *gay men*, *bisexual men*, and *bisexual women* are preferable to *homosexual* when one is referring to people who identify this way. *Lesbian*, *gay*, and *bisexual* refer primarily to identities and to the culture and communities that have developed among people who share those identities. As such, the terms *lesbians*, *gay men*, and *bisexual individuals* are more accurate than *homosexual*. Furthermore, the term *homosexuality* has been and continues to be associated with negative stereotypes, pathology, and the reduction of people's identities to their sexual behavior. *Gay* can be interpreted broadly, to include men and women, or more narrowly, to include only men.

1.14 Racial and Ethnic Identity

Preferences for terms referring to racial and ethnic groups change often. One reason for this is simply personal preference; preferred designations are as varied as the people they name. Another reason is that over time, designations can become dated and sometimes negative. Authors are reminded of the two basic guidelines of specificity and sensitivity. In keeping with Guideline 2, use commonly accepted designations (e.g., Census categories) while being sensitive to participants' preferred designation. For example, some North American people of African ancestry prefer *Black* and others prefer *African American*; both terms currently are acceptable. On the other hand, *Negro* and *Afro-American* have become dated; therefore, usage of these terms generally is inappropriate. In keeping with Guideline 1, precision is important in the description of your sample (see the *Publication Manual*, APA, 2010, section 2.06); in general, use the more specific rather than the less specific term.

Language that essentializes or reifies race is strongly discouraged and is generally considered inappropriate. For example, phrases such as *the Black race* and *the White race* are essentialist in nature, portray human groups monolithically, and often serve to perpetuate stereotypes. Authors sometimes use the word *minority* as a proxy for non-White racial and ethnic groups. This usage may be viewed pejoratively because *minority* is usually equated with being less than, oppressed, and deficient in comparison with the majority (i.e., Whites). Use a modifier (such as *ethnic* or *racial*) when using the word *minority*. When possible, use the actual name of the group or groups to which you are referring.

Racial and ethnic groups are designated by proper nouns and are capitalized. Therefore, use *Black* and *White* instead of *black* and *white* (the use of colors to refer to other human groups currently is considered pejorative and should not be used). Unparallel designations (e.g., *African Americans* and *Whites*; *Asian Americans* and *Black Americans*) should be avoided because one group is described by color while the other group is described by cultural heritage. For modifiers, do not use hyphens in multiword names, even if the names act as unit modifiers (e.g., *Asian American* participants).

Designations for some ethnic groups are described next. These groups frequently are included in studies published in APA journals. These examples are far from exhaustive but illustrate some of the complexities of naming (see the Guidelines for Unbiased Language at www.apastyle.org). Depending on where a person is from, individuals may prefer to be called *Hispanic*, *Latino*, *Chicano*, or some other designation; *Hispanic* is not necessarily an all-encompassing term, and authors should consult with their participants. In general, naming a nation or region of origin is helpful (e.g., *Cuban*, *Salvadoran*, or *Guatemalan* is more specific than *Central American* or *Hispanic*).

American Indian, *Native American*, and *Native North American* are all accepted terms for referring to indigenous peoples of North America. When referring to groups including Hawaiians and Samoans, you may use the broader designation *Native Americans*. The indigenous peoples of Canada may be referred to as *First Nations* or *Inuit* people. There are close to 450 Native North American groups, and authors are encouraged to name the participants' specific groups, recognizing that some groups prefer the name for their group in their native language (e.g., *Dine* instead of *Navajo*, *Tohono O'odham* instead of *Papago*).

The term *Asian* or *Asian American* is preferred to the older term *Oriental*. It is generally useful to specify the name of the Asian subgroup: Chinese, Vietnamese, Korean, Pakistani, and so on. People of Middle Eastern descent may also be identified by nation of origin: Iraqi, Lebanese, and so forth.

1.15 Disabilities

The overall principle for "nonhandicapping" language is to maintain the integrity (worth) of all individuals as human beings. Avoid language that objectifies a person by her or his condition (e.g., *autistic*, *neurotic*), that uses pictorial metaphors (e.g., *wheelchair bound* or *confined to a wheelchair*), that uses excessive and negative labels (e.g., *AIDS victim*, *brain damaged*), or that can be regarded as a slur (e.g., *cripple*, *invalid*). Use people-first language, and do not focus on the individual's disabling or chronic condition (e.g., *person with paraplegia*, *youth with autism*). Also use people-first language to describe groups of people with disabilities. For instance, say *people with intellectual disabilities* in contrast to *the retarded* (University of Kansas, Research and Training Center on Independent Living, 2008).

Avoid euphemisms that are condescending when describing individuals with disabilities (e.g., *special, physically challenged, handi-capable*). Some people with disabilities consider these terms patronizing and offensive. When writing about populations with disabilities or participants, emphasize both capabilities and concerns to avoid reducing them to a "bundle of deficiencies" (Rappaport, 1977). Do not refer to individuals with disabilities as *patients* or *cases* unless the context is within a hospital or clinical setting.

1.16 Age

Age should be reported as part of the description of participants in the Method section. Be specific in providing age ranges; avoid open-ended definitions such as "under 18 years" or "over 65 years." *Girl* and *boy* are correct terms for referring to individuals under the age of 12 years. *Young man* and *young woman* and *female adolescent* and *male adolescent* may be used for individuals aged 13 to 17 years. For persons 18 years and older, use *women* and *men*. The terms *elderly* and *senior* are not acceptable as nouns; some may consider their use as adjectives pejorative. Generational descriptors such as *boomer* or *baby boomer* should not be used unless they are related to a study on this topic. The term *older adults* is preferred. Age groups may also be described with adjectives. Gerontologists may prefer to use combination terms for older age groups (*young-old, old-old, very old, oldest old*, and *centenarians*); provide the specific ages of these groups and use them only as adjectives. Use *dementia* instead of *senility*; specify the type of dementia when known (e.g., *dementia of the Alzheimer's type*). For more references relating to age, see *Guidelines for the Evaluation of Dementia and Age-Related Cognitive Decline* (APA Presidential Task Force on the Assessment of Age-Consistent Memory Decline and Dementia, 1998) and "Guidelines for Psychological Practice With Older Adults" (APA, 2004; see also www.apastyle.org).

1.17 Historical and Interpretive Inaccuracies

Authors are encouraged to avoid perpetuating demeaning attitudes and biased assumptions about people in their writing. At the same time, authors need to avoid historical and interpretive inaccuracies. Historians and scholars writing literature reviews must be careful not to misrepresent ideas of the past in an effort to avoid language bias. Changes in nouns and pronouns may result in serious misrepresentation of the original author's ideas and give a false interpretation of that author's beliefs and intentions. In such writing, it is best to retain the original language and to comment on it in the discussion. Quotations should not be changed to accommodate current sensibilities.

Contemporary authors may indicate a historical author's original term by following it with an asterisk the first time it appears and by providing historical context directly following the quotation. Below is an example of historically appropriate use of a term that is considered biased by today's standards.

> In forming the elite scientific society called the Experimentalists, Titchener "wanted above all to have free, informal interchange between older and younger men* in the area of experimental psychology, with the goal of socializing the next generation into the profession" (Furumoto, 1988, p. 105).

*In this example, the term *men* seems to convey Titchener's intention to exclude women from the society. Substituting a more gender-neutral or inclusive term may be historically inaccurate.

Grammar and Usage

Incorrect grammar and careless construction of sentences distract the reader, introduce ambiguity, and generally obstruct communication. The examples in this section represent problems of grammar and usage that occur frequently in manuscripts received by journal editors.

1.18 Verbs

Verbs are vigorous, direct communicators. Use the active rather than the passive voice, and select tense or mood carefully.

Prefer the active voice.

Preferred:

> We conducted the survey in a controlled setting.

Nonpreferred:

> The survey was conducted in a controlled setting.

The passive voice is acceptable in expository writing and when you want to focus on the object or recipient of the action rather than on the actor. For example, "The speakers were attached to either side of the chair" emphasizes the placement of speakers, not who placed them—the more appropriate focus in the Method section. "The President was shot" emphasizes the importance of the person shot.

Select tense carefully. Use the past tense to express an action or a condition that occurred at a specific, definite time in the past, as when discussing another researcher's work and when reporting your results.

Correct:

> Sanchez (2000) presented similar results.

Incorrect:

> Sanchez (2000) presents similar results.

Use the present perfect tense to express a past action or condition that did not occur at a specific, definite time or to describe an action beginning in the past and continuing to the present.

Correct:

> Since that time, several investigators have used this method.

Incorrect:

> Since that time, several investigators used this method.

Select the appropriate mood. Use the subjunctive only to describe conditions that are contrary to fact or improbable; do not use the subjunctive to describe simple conditions or contingencies.

Correct:

> If the experiment were not designed this way, the results could not be interpreted properly.

Incorrect:

> If the experiment was not designed this way, the results could not be interpreted properly.

Use *would* with care. *Would* can correctly be used to mean *habitually*, as "The child would walk about the classroom," or to express a conditional action, as "We would sign the letter if we could." Do not use *would* to hedge; for example, change *it would appear that* to *it appears that*.

1.19 Agreement of Subject and Verb

A verb must agree in number (i.e., singular or plural) with its subject, regardless of intervening phrases that begin with such words as *together with*, *including*, *plus*, and *as well as*.

Correct:

> The percentage of correct responses as well as the speed of the responses increases with practice.

Incorrect:

> The percentage of correct responses as well as the speed of the responses increase with practice.

The plural form of some nouns of foreign origin, particularly those that end in the letter *a*, may appear to be singular and can cause authors to select a verb that does not agree in number with the noun.

Correct:

The data indicate that Terrence was correct.

Incorrect:

The data indicates that Terrence was correct.

Correct:

The phenomena occur every 100 years.

Incorrect:

The phenomena occurs every 100 years.

Consult a dictionary (APA prefers *Merriam-Webster's Collegiate Dictionary*, 2005) when in doubt about the plural form of nouns of foreign origin. See www.apastyle.org for examples with collective nouns.

1.20 Pronouns

Pronouns replace nouns. Each pronoun should refer clearly to its antecedent and should agree with the antecedent in number and gender.

A pronoun must agree in number (i.e., singular or plural) with the noun it replaces.

Correct:

Neither the highest scorer nor the lowest scorer in the group had any doubt about his or her competence.

Incorrect:

Neither the highest scorer nor the lowest scorer in the group had any doubt about their competence.

A pronoun must agree in gender (i.e., masculine, feminine, or neuter) with the noun it replaces. This rule extends to relative pronouns (pronouns that link subordinate clauses to nouns). Use *who* for human beings; use *that* or *which* for nonhuman animals and for things.

Correct:

> The students who completed the task successfully were rewarded.

Correct:

> The instructions that were included in the experiment were complex.

Incorrect:

> The students that completed the task successfully were rewarded.

Use neuter pronouns to refer to animals (e.g., "the dog . . . it") unless the animals have been named:

> The chimps were tested daily. . . . Sheba was tested unrestrained in an open testing area, which was her usual context for training and testing.

Pronouns can be subjects or objects of verbs or prepositions. Use *who* as the subject of a verb and *whom* as the object of a verb or a preposition. You can determine whether a relative pronoun is the subject or object of a verb by turning the subordinate clause around and substituting a personal pronoun. If you can substitute *he* or *she*, *who* is correct; if you can substitute *him* or *her*, *whom* is correct.

Correct:

> Name the participant who you found achieved scores above the median. [You found *he* or *she* achieved scores above the median.]

Incorrect:

> Name the participant whom you found achieved scores above the median. [You found *him* or *her* achieved scores above the median.]

Correct:

> The participant whom I identified as the youngest dropped out. [I identified *him* or *her* as the youngest.]

Incorrect:

> The participant who I identified as the youngest dropped out. [I identified *he* or *she* as the youngest.]

In a phrase consisting of a pronoun or noun plus a present participle (e.g., *running*, *flying*) that is used as an object of a preposition, the participle can be either a noun or a modifier of a noun, depending on the intended meaning. When you use a participle as a noun, make the other pronoun or noun possessive.

Correct:

> We had nothing to do with their being the winners.

Incorrect:

> We had nothing to do with them being the winners.

Correct:

> The result is questionable because of one participant's performing at very high speed. [The result is questionable because of the performance, not because of the participant.]

Incorrect:

> The result is questionable because of one participant performing at very high speed.

1.21 Misplaced and Dangling Modifiers and Use of Adverbs

An adjective or an adverb, whether a single word or a phrase, must clearly refer to the word it modifies.

Misplaced modifiers. Because of their placement in a sentence, misplaced modifiers ambiguously or illogically modify a word. You can eliminate misplaced modifiers by placing an adjective or an adverb as close as possible to the word it modifies.

Correct:

> Using this procedure, the investigator tested the participants.

Correct:

> The investigator tested the participants who were using the procedure.

Incorrect:

> The investigator tested the participants using this procedure. [The sentence is unclear about whether the investigator or the participants used this procedure.]

Correct:

> On the basis of this assumption, we developed a model. . . .

Correct:

> Based on this assumption, the model. . . . ,

Incorrect:

> Based on this assumption, we developed a model. . . . [This construction says, "We are based on an assumption."]

Many writers have trouble with the word *only*. Place *only* next to the word or phrase it modifies.

Correct:

> These data provide only a partial answer.

Incorrect:

> These data only provide a partial answer.

Dangling modifiers. Dangling modifiers have no referent in the sentence. Many of these result from the use of the passive voice. By writing in the active voice, you can avoid many dangling modifiers.

Correct:

> Using this procedure, I tested the participants. [I, not the participants, used the procedure.]

Incorrect:

> The participants were tested using this procedure.

Correct:

> Mulholland and Williams (2000) found that this group performed better, a result that is congruent with those of other studies. [The result, not Mulholland and Williams, is congruent.]

Incorrect:

> Congruent with other studies, Mulholland and Williams (2000) found that this group performed better.

Adverbs. Adverbs can be used as introductory or transitional words. Adverbs modify verbs, adjectives, and other adverbs and express manner or quality. Some adverbs, however—such as *fortunately*, *similarly*, *certainly*, *consequently*, *conversely*, and *regrettably*—can also be used as introductory or transitional words as long as the sense is confined to, for example, "it is fortunate that" or "in a similar manner." Use adverbs judiciously as introductory or transitional words. Ask yourself whether the introduction or transition is needed and whether the adverb is being used correctly.

Some of the more common introductory adverbial phrases are *importantly*, *more importantly*, *interestingly*, and *firstly*. Although *importantly* is used widely, whether its adverbial usage is proper is debatable. Both *importantly* and *interestingly* can often be recast to enhance the message of a sentence or simply be omitted without a loss of meaning.

Correct:

> More important, the total amount of available long-term memory activation, and not the rate of spreading activation, drives the rate and probability of retrieval.

Correct:

> Expressive behavior and autonomic nervous system activity also have figured importantly. . . .

Incorrect:

> More importantly, the total amount of available long-term memory activation, and not the rate of

spreading activation, drives the rate and probability of retrieval.

Correct:

We were surprised to learn that the total. . . .

We find it interesting that the total. . . .

An interesting finding was that. . . .

Incorrect:

Interestingly, the total amount of available long-term memory activation, and not the rate of spreading activation, drives the rate and probability of retrieval.

Correct:

First, we hypothesized that the quality of the therapeutic alliance would be rated higher. . . .

Incorrect:

Firstly, we hypothesized that the quality of the therapeutic alliance would be rated higher. . . .

Another adverb often misused as an introductory or transitional word is *hopefully*. *Hopefully* means "in a hopeful manner" or "full of hope"; *hopefully* should not be used to mean "I hope" or "it is hoped."

Correct:

I hope this is not the case.

Incorrect:

Hopefully, this is not the case.

1.22 Relative Pronouns and Subordinate Conjunctions

Relative pronouns (*who, whom, that, which*) and subordinate conjunctions (e.g., *since, while, although*) introduce an element that is subordinate to the main clause of the sentence and reflect the relationship of the subordinate element to the main clause. Therefore, select these pronouns and conjunctions with care; interchanging them may reduce the precision of your meaning.

Relative pronouns.

That *versus* which. *That* clauses (called *restrictive*) are essential to the meaning of the sentence:

> The materials that worked well in the first experiment were used in the second experiment.

Which clauses can merely add further information (*nonrestrictive*) or can be essential to the meaning (restrictive) of the sentence. APA prefers to reserve *which* for nonrestrictive clauses and use *that* in restrictive clauses.

Restrictive:

> The cards that worked well in the first experiment were not useful in the second experiment. [Only those cards that worked well in the first experiment were not useful in the second; prefer *that*.]

Nonrestrictive:

> The cards, which worked well in the first experiment, were not useful in the second experiment. [The second experiment was not appropriate for the cards.]

Consistent use of *that* for restrictive clauses and *which* for nonrestrictive clauses, which are set off with commas, will help make your writing clear and precise.

Subordinate conjunctions.

While *and* since. Some style authorities accept the use of *while* and *since* when they do not refer strictly to time; however, words like these, with more than one meaning, can cause confusion. Because precision and clarity are the standards in scientific writing, restricting your use of *while* and *since* to their temporal meanings is helpful. The following examples illustrate the temporal meanings of these terms:

> Bragg (1965) found that participants performed well while listening to music.

Several versions of the test have been developed since the test was first introduced.

While *versus* although, and, or but. Use *while* to link events occurring simultaneously; otherwise, use *although*, *and*, or *but* in place of *while*.

Precise:

Although these findings are unusual, they are not unique.

Imprecise:

While these findings are unusual, they are not unique.

Precise:

The argument is purely philosophical, but the conclusion can also yield an empirical hypothesis, amenable to empirical investigation.

Imprecise:

While the argument is purely philosophical, the conclusion can also yield an empirical hypothesis, amenable to empirical investigation.

Since *versus* because. *Since* is more precise when it is used to refer only to time (to mean "after that"); otherwise, replace it with *because*.

Precise:

Data for two participants were incomplete because these participants did not report for follow-up testing.

Imprecise:

Data for two participants were incomplete since these participants did not report for follow-up testing.

1.23 Parallel Construction

To enhance the reader's understanding, present parallel ideas in parallel or coordinate form. Make certain that all elements of the parallelism are present before and after the coordinating conjunction (i.e., *and, but, or, nor*).

Correct:

The results show that such changes could be made without affecting error rate and that latencies continued to decrease over time.

Incorrect:

The results show that such changes could be made without affecting error rate and latencies continued to decrease over time.

With coordinating conjunctions used in pairs (*between . . . and, both . . . and, neither . . . nor, either . . . or, not only . . . but also*), place the first conjunction immediately before the first part of the parallelism.

Between and *and.*

Correct:

We recorded the difference between the performance of subjects who completed the first task and the performance of those who completed the second task. [The difference is between the subjects' performances, not between the performance and the task.]

Incorrect:

We recorded the difference between the performance of subjects who completed the first task and the second task.

Correct:

between 2.5 and 4.0 years of age

Incorrect:

between 2.5–4.0 years of age

Both and *and.*

Correct:

> The names were difficult both to pronounce and to spell.

Incorrect:

> The names were both difficult to pronounce and spell.

Never use *both* with *as well as*: The resulting construction is redundant.

Correct:

> The names were difficult to pronounce as well as to spell.

Incorrect:

> The names were difficult both to pronounce as well as to spell.

Neither and *nor*; *either* and *or.*

Correct:

> Neither the responses to the auditory stimuli nor the responses to the tactile stimuli were repeated.

Incorrect:

> Neither the responses to the auditory stimuli nor to the tactile stimuli were repeated.

Correct:

> The respondents either gave the worst answer or gave the best answer.

or

> The respondents gave either the worst answer or the best answer.

Incorrect:

> The respondents either gave the worst answer or the best answer.

Not only and *but also.*

Correct:

It is surprising not only that pencil-and-paper scores predicted this result but also that all other predictors were less accurate.

Incorrect:

It is not only surprising that pencil-and-paper scores predicted this result but also that all other predictors were less accurate.

Elements in a series should also be parallel in form.

Correct:

The participants were told to make themselves comfortable, to read the instructions, and to ask about anything they did not understand.

Incorrect:

The participants were told to make themselves comfortable, to read the instructions, and that they should ask about anything they did not understand.

Take care to use parallel structure in lists and in table stubs (see sections 1.04 and 5.13).

2

Punctuation, Spelling, and Capitalization

When editors refer to *style*, they mean the rules or guidelines a publisher observes to ensure clear, consistent presentation in scholarly articles. Authors follow the style rules established by the publisher to avoid inconsistencies among journal articles or book chapters. For example, without rules of style, three different manuscripts might use *sub-test*, *subtest*, and *Subtest* in one issue of a journal or in one book. Although the meaning of the word is the same and the choice of one style over the other may seem arbitrary (in this case, *subtest* is APA Style), such variations in style may distract or confuse the reader.

This chapter describes the style for APA journals regarding punctuation, spelling, and capitalization. It omits general rules explained in widely available style manuals and examples of usage with little relevance to APA journals. Style manuals agree more often than they disagree; where they disagree, the *Publication Manual of the American Psychological Association* (APA, 2010) takes precedence for APA publications.

Punctuation

Punctuation establishes the cadence of a sentence, telling the reader where to pause (comma, semicolon, and colon), stop (period and question mark), or take a detour (dash, parentheses, and brackets). Punctuation of a sentence usually denotes a pause in thought; different kinds of punctuation indicate different kinds and lengths of pauses.

2.01 Spacing After Punctuation Marks

Insert one space after

- commas, colons, and semicolons;
- periods that separate parts of a reference citation; and
- periods of the initials in personal names (e.g., J. R. Zhang).

Exception: Do not insert a space after internal periods in abbreviations (e.g., a.m., i.e., U.S.), including identity-concealing labels for study participants (F.I.M.), or around colons in ratios. Spacing twice after punctuation marks at the end of a sentence aids readers of draft manuscripts.

2.02 Period

Use a period to end a complete sentence. Periods are used with abbreviations as follows:

Use periods with

- initials of names (J. R. Smith).
- abbreviation for United States when it is used as an adjective (U.S. Navy).
- identity-concealing labels for study participants (F.I.M.). (See section 2.01 on spacing.)
- Latin abbreviations (a.m., cf., i.e., vs.).
- reference abbreviations (Vol. 1, 2nd ed., p. 6, F. Supp.).

Do not use periods with

- abbreviations of state names (NY; OH; Washington, DC) in reference list entries or in vendor locations (e.g., for drugs and apparatus described in the Method section).

■ capital letter abbreviations and acronyms (APA, NDA, NIMH, IQ).

■ abbreviations for routes of administration (icv, im, ip, iv, sc).

■ web addresses in text or in the reference list (http://www.apa.org). In text, include these in parentheses when possible or revise the sentence to avoid ending a sentence with a URL and no punctuation.

■ metric and nonmetric measurement abbreviations (cd, cm, ft, hr, kg, lb, min, ml, s).

Exception: The abbreviation for inch (in.) takes a period because without the period it could be misread.

2.03 Comma

Use a comma

■ between elements (including before *and* and *or*) in a series of three or more items.

> *Correct:*
>> the height, width, or depth
>> in a study by Stacy, Newcomb, and Bentler (1991)
>
> *Incorrect:*
>> in a study by Stacy, Newcomb and Bentler (1991)

■ to set off a nonessential or nonrestrictive clause, that is, a clause that embellishes a sentence but if removed would leave the grammatical structure and meaning of the sentence intact.

> Switch A, which was on a panel, controlled the recording device.
>
> Statistically significant differences were found for both ratings of controllability by self, $F(3, 132) = 19.58$, $p < .001$, est $\eta^2 = .31$, 95% CI [.17, .43], and ratings of controllability by others, $F(3, 96) = 3.21$, $p = .026$, est $\eta^2 = .09$, [.00, .20].

■ to separate two independent clauses joined by a conjunction.

> Cedar shavings covered the floor, and paper was available for shredding and nest building.

■ to set off the year in exact dates.

> April 18, 1992, was the correct date.

but

> April 1992 was the correct month.

■ to set off the year in parenthetical reference citations.

> (Patrick, 1993)

> (Kelsey, 1993, discovered . . .)

■ to separate groups of three digits in most numbers of 1,000 or more (see section 4.07 for exceptions).

Do not use a comma

■ before an essential or restrictive clause, that is, a clause that limits or defines the material it modifies. Removal of such a clause from the sentence would alter the intended meaning.

> The switch that stops the recording device also controls the light.

■ between the two parts of a compound predicate.

> *Correct:*
> All subjects completed the first phase of the experiment and returned the following week for Phase 2.

> *Incorrect:*
> All subjects completed the first phase of the experiment, and returned the following week for Phase 2.

■ to separate parts of measurement.

> 8 years 2 months   3 min 40 s

2.04 Semicolon

Use a semicolon

■ to separate two independent clauses that are not joined by a conjunction.

> The participants in the first study were paid; those in the second were unpaid.

■ to separate elements in a series that already contain commas. (See section 1.04 for the use of semicolons in numbered or lettered series.)

> The color order was red, yellow, blue; blue, yellow, red; or yellow, red, blue.

> (Davis & Hueter, 1994; Pettigrew, 1993)

> age, $M = 34.5$ years, 95% CI [29.4, 39.6]; years of education, $M = 10.4$ [8.7, 12.1]; and weekly income, $M = 612$ [522, 702];

2.05 Colon

Use a colon

■ between a grammatically complete introductory clause (one that could stand as a sentence) and a final phrase or clause that illustrates, extends, or amplifies the preceding thought. If the clause following the colon is a complete sentence, it begins with a capital letter.

> For example, Freud (1930/1961) wrote of two urges: an urge toward union with others and an egoistic urge toward happiness.

> They have agreed on the outcome: Informed participants perform better than do uninformed participants.

■ in ratios and proportions.

> The proportion (saltwater) was 1:8.

■ in references between place of publication and publisher.

> New York, NY: Wiley.   St. Louis, MO: Mosby.

Do not use a colon

■ after an introduction that is not an independent clause or complete sentence.

> The formula is $r_i = a_i + e$.

> The instructions for the task were

>> Your group's task is to rank the 15 items in terms of their importance for the crew's survival.

2.06 Dash

Use a dash to indicate only a sudden interruption in the continuity of a sentence. Overuse weakens the flow of material. (See also section 2.16 for capitalization following dashes in titles.)

> These two participants—one from the first group and one from the second—were tested separately.

2.07 Typing Hyphens, Dashes, and Minus Signs

Hyphens, dashes, and minus signs are each typed differently.

■ **hyphen:** Use no space before or after (e.g., trial-by-trial analysis).

■ **em dash:** An em dash is longer than a hyphen or an en dash and is used to set off an element added to amplify or to digress from the main clause (e.g., Studies—published and unpublished—are included). Use no space before or after an em dash. If an em dash is not available on your keyboard, use two hyphens with no space before or after.

■ **en dash:** An en dash is longer and thinner than a hyphen yet shorter than an em dash and is used between words of equal weight in a compound adjective (e.g., Chicago–London flight). Type as an en dash or, if the en dash is not available on your keyboard, as a single hyphen. In either case, use no space before or after.

■ **minus sign:** A typeset minus sign is the same length as an en dash, but it is slightly thicker and slightly higher. If a minus sign is not available in your word-processing program, use a hyphen with a space on both sides (e.g., a - b). For a negative value, use a hyphen rather than a minus sign, with a space before but no space after (e.g., -5.25).

2.08 Quotation Marks

Observe the following guidelines for uses of double quotation marks other than in material quoted directly from a source.

Use double quotation marks

■ to introduce a word or phrase used as an ironic comment, as slang, or as an invented or coined expression. Use quotation marks the first time the word or phrase is used; thereafter, do not use quotation marks.

Correct:

considered "normal" behavior

the "good-outcome" variable . . . the good-outcome variable [no quotation marks after the initial usage]

Incorrect:

considered 'normal' behavior

the "good-outcome" variable . . . the "good-outcome" variable

■ to set off the title of an article or chapter in a periodical or book when the title is mentioned in text.

> Riger's (1992) article, "Epistemological Debates, Feminist Voices: Science, Social Values, and the Study of Women"

■ to reproduce material from a test item or verbatim instructions to participants.

> The first fill-in item was "could be expected to _____."

If instructions are long, set them off from text in a block format without quotation marks. (See sections 2.09 and 7.03 for discussion of block format.)

Do not use double quotation marks

■ to identify the anchors of a scale. Instead, italicize them.

> We ranked the items on a scale ranging from 1 (*all of the time*) to 5 (*never*).

■ to cite a letter, word, phrase, or sentence as a linguistic example. Instead, italicize the term.

> He clarified the distinction between *farther* and *further.*

■ to introduce a technical or key term. Instead, italicize the term.

> The term *zero-base budgeting* appeared frequently in the speech.

> She compared it with *meta-analysis,* which is described in the next section.

■ to hedge. Do not use any punctuation with such expressions.

> *Correct:*
> The teacher rewarded the class with tokens.
> *Incorrect:*
> The teacher "rewarded" the class with tokens.

2.09 Double or Single Quotation Marks

In text. Use double quotation marks to enclose quotations in text. Use single quotation marks within double quotation marks to set off material that in the original source was enclosed in double quotation marks.

Correct:

> Miele (1993) found that "the 'placebo effect,' which had been verified in previous studies, disappeared when [only the first group's] behaviors were studied in this manner" (p. 276).

Incorrect:

> "Miele (1993) found that "the "placebo effect," which had been verified in previous studies, disappeared when [only the first group's] behaviors were studied in this manner" (p. 276).

In block quotations (any quotations of 40 or more words). Do not use quotation marks to enclose block quotations. Do use double quotation marks to enclose any quoted material within a block quotation.

Correct:

> Miele (1993) found the following:
>
> > The "placebo effect," which had been verified in previous studies, disappeared when behaviors were studied in this manner. Furthermore, the behaviors *were never exhibited again* [emphasis added], even when reel [*sic*] drugs were administered. Earlier studies (e.g., Abdullah, 1984; Fox, 1979) were clearly premature in attributing the results to a placebo effect. (p. 276)

Incorrect:

> Miele (1993) found the following:
>
> > "The 'placebo effect,' which had been verified in previous studies, disappeared when behaviors were studied in this manner. Furthermore, the behaviors *were never exhibited again* [emphasis added], even when reel [*sic*] drugs were administered. Earlier studies (e.g., Abdullah, 1984;

Fox, 1979) were clearly premature in attributing
the results to a placebo effect (p. 276)."

With other punctuation. Place periods and commas within
closing single or double quotation marks. Place other
punctuation marks inside quotation marks only when
they are part of the quoted material.

2.10 Parentheses

Use parentheses

■ to set off structurally independent elements.

The patterns were statistically significant (see
Figure 5).

(When a complete sentence is enclosed in parentheses, place punctuation in the sentence inside
the parentheses, like this.) If only part of a sentence is enclosed in parentheses (like this), place
punctuation outside the parentheses (like this).

■ to set off reference citations in text (see sections
7.09–7.21 and Appendix 8.1 for further discussion of
reference citations in text).

Dumas and Dore (1991) reported

is fully described elsewhere (Hong & O'Neil,
1992) in the *Diagnostic and Statistical Manual of
Mental Disorders* (4th ed., text rev.; *DSM–IV–TR*;
American Psychiatric Association, 2000)

■ to introduce an abbreviation.

effect on the galvanic skin response (GSR)

■ to set off letters that identify items in a series within a sentence or paragraph (see also section 1.04 on seriation).

The subject areas included (a) synonyms associated with cultural interactions, (b) descriptors for
ethnic group membership, and (c) psychological

symptoms and outcomes associated with bicultural adaptation.

- to group mathematical expressions (see also sections 2.11 and 4.17).

    $(k-1)/(g-2)$

- to enclose the citation or page number of a direct quotation (see also section 7.03).

    The author stated, "The effect disappeared within minutes" (Lopez, 1993, p. 311), but she did not say which effect.

    Lopez (1993) found that "the effect disappeared within minutes" (p. 311), but she did not say which effect.

- to enclose numbers that identify displayed formulas and equations.

    $$M_j = \alpha M_{j-1} + f_j + g_j * g_{j'} \tag{1}$$

- to enclose statistical values.

    was statistically significant $(p = .031)$

- to enclose degrees of freedom.

    $t(75) = 2.19$

    $F(2, 116) = 3.71$

Do not use parentheses

- to enclose material within other parentheses.

    (the Beck Depression Inventory [BDI]) [Use brackets to avoid nested parentheses.]

    were statistically different, $F(4, 132) = 13.62$, $p < .001$. [Use a comma before the statistics to avoid nested parentheses.]

■ back to back.

> *Correct:*
>> (e.g., defensive pessimism; Norem & Cantor, 1986)

> *Incorrect:*
>> (e.g., defensive pessimism) (Norem & Cantor, 1986)

2.11 Brackets

Use brackets

■ to enclose the values that are the limits of a confidence interval

> 95% CIs [−7.2, 4.3], [9.2, 12.4], and [−1.2, −0.5]

■ to enclose material inserted in a quotation by some person other than the original writer.

> "when [his own and others'] behaviors were studied" (Hanisch, 1992, p. 24)

■ to enclose parenthetical material that is already within parentheses.

> (The results for the control group [$n = 8$] are also presented in Figure 2.)

Exception 1: Do not use brackets if the material can be set off easily with commas without confounding meaning.

> (as Imai, 1990, later concluded)

not

> (as Imai [1990] later concluded)

Exception 2: In mathematical material, the placement of brackets and parentheses is reversed; that is, parentheses appear within brackets. (See section 4.17 for further discussion of brackets in equations.)

Do not use brackets

■ to set off statistics that already include parentheses.

> *Correct:*
>> was statistically significant, $F(l, 32) = 4.37$, $p = .045$.
>
> *Incorrect:*
>> was statistically significant ($F[l, 32] = 4.37$, $p = .045$).
>
> *Incorrect:*
>> was statistically significant [$F(l, 32) = 4.37$, $p = .045$].

2.12 Slash

Use a slash (also called a *virgule*, *solidus*, or *shill*)

■ to clarify a relationship in which a hyphenated compound is used.

> the classification/similarity-judgment condition
>
> hits/false-alarms comparison

■ to separate numerator from denominator.

> X/Y

■ to indicate *per* to separate units of measurement accompanied by a numerical value (see section 3.08).

> 0.5 deg/s   7.4 mg/kg
>
> *but*
>
> luminance is measured in candelas per square meter

■ to set off English phonemes.

> /o/

■ to cite a republished work in text.

> Freud (1923/1961)

Do not use a slash

■ when a phrase would be clearer.

> Each child handed the ball to her mother or
> guardian.

not

> Each child handed the ball to her mother/guardian.

■ for simple comparisons. Use a hyphen or short dash
(en dash) instead.

> test–retest reliability

not

> test/retest reliability

■ more than once to express compound units. Use centered dots and parentheses as needed to prevent ambiguity.

> $nmol \bullet hr^{-1} \bullet mg^{-1}$

not

> nmol/hr/mg

Spelling
2.13 Preferred Spelling

Spelling should conform to standard American English as
exemplified in *Merriam-Webster's Collegiate Dictionary*
(2005), the standard spelling reference for APA journals
and books; spelling of psychological terms should conform to the *APA Dictionary of Psychology* (VandenBos,
2007). If a word is not in *Webster's Collegiate*, consult the
more comprehensive *Webster's Third New International
Dictionary* (2002). If the dictionary gives a choice, use the
first spelling listed; for example, use *aging* and *canceled*
rather than *ageing* and *cancelled*.

Plural forms of some words of Latin or Greek origin
can be troublesome; a list of preferred spellings of some

of the more common ones follows. Authors are reminded that plural nouns take plural verbs.

Singular	Plural
appendix	appendices
cannula	cannulas
datum	data
phenomenon	phenomena

In general, the possessive of a singular name is formed by adding an apostrophe and an *s*, even when a name ends in *s*; the possessive of a plural name is formed by adding an apostrophe. A list of examples follows as well as some exceptions.

Singular	Plural
Freud's	the Freuds'
James's	the Jameses'
Watson's	the Watsons'
Skinner's	the Skinners'

Exceptions: Use an apostrophe only with the singular form of names ending in unpronounced *s* (e.g., Descartes'). It is preferable to include *of* when referring to the plural form of names ending in unpronounced *s* (e.g., the home of the Descartes).

2.14 Hyphenation

Compound words take many forms; that is, two words may be written as (a) two separate words; (b) a hyphenated word; or (c) one unbroken, "solid" word. Choosing the proper form is sometimes frustrating. For example, is *follow up*, *follow-up*, or *followup* the form to be used? The dictionary is an excellent guide for such decisions, especially for nonscientific words (the term is *follow-up* when functioning as a noun or adjective but *follow up* when functioning as a verb). When a compound can be found in the dictionary, its usage is established and it is known as a *permanent compound* (e.g., *high school*, *caregiver*, and *self-esteem*). Dictionaries do not always agree on the way a compound should be written (open, solid, or hyphenated); APA follows *Webster's Collegiate* in most cases. Compound terms are often introduced into the language as separate or hyphenated words, and as they become more commonplace, they tend to fuse into a solid word. For example, the hyphen was dropped from *life-style* in the 11th edition of *Webster's Collegiate*, and *data base* is now *database*.

There is another kind of compound—the *temporary compound*—which is made up of two or more words that occur together, perhaps only in a particular paper, to express a thought. Because language is constantly expanding, especially in science, temporary compounds develop that are not yet listed in the dictionary. If a temporary compound modifies another word, it may or may not be hyphenated, depending on (a) its position in the sentence and (b) whether the pairing of a compound with another word can cause the reader to misinterpret meaning. The main rule to remember is that if a temporary compound precedes what it modifies, it may need to be hyphenated, and if it follows what it modifies, it usually does not. If a compound is not in the dictionary, follow the general principles of hyphenation given here and in Table 2.1. If you are still in doubt, use hyphens for clarity rather than omitting them. (See also Tables 2.2 and 2.3 for treatment of prefixes and suffixes.)

General Principle 1

If a compound adjective can be misread, use a hyphen.

General Principle 2

In a temporary compound that is used as an adjective before a noun, use a hyphen if the term can be misread or if the term expresses a single thought (i.e., all words together modify the noun). For example, are *different word lists* (a) word lists that are different from other word lists (if so, *different* modifies *word lists*; thus, write *different word lists*) or (b) lists that present different words (if so, the first word modifies the second, and together they

Table 2.1. Guide to Hyphenating Terms

Rule	Example
Hyphenate	
1. A compound with a participle when it precedes the term it modifies	■ role-playing technique ■ anxiety-arousing condition ■ water-deprived animals
2. A phrase used as an adjective when it precedes the term it modifies	■ trial-by-trial analysis ■ to-be-recalled items ■ all-or-none questionnaire
3. An adjective-and-noun compound when it precedes the term it modifies	■ high-anxiety group ■ middle-class families ■ low-frequency words
4. A compound with a number as the first element when the compound precedes the term it modifies	■ two-way ANOVA ■ six-trial problem ■ 16-s interval
5. A fraction used as an adjective	■ two-thirds majority
Do not hyphenate	
1. A compound including an adverb ending in *ly*	■ widely used text ■ randomly assigned groups
2. A compound including a comparative or superlative adjective	■ better written paper ■ less informed interviewers ■ higher scoring students
3. Chemical terms	■ sodium chloride solution ■ amino acid compound
4. Foreign phrases used as adjectives or adverbs	■ a posteriori test ■ post hoc comparisons
5. A modifier including a letter or numeral as the second element	■ Group B participants ■ Type II error ■ Trial 1 performance
6. Common fractions used as nouns	■ one third of the participants

Table 2.2. Prefixes and Suffixes That Do Not Require Hyphens

Prefix or suffix	Example	Prefix or suffix	Example
able	retrievable	mini	minisession
after	aftereffect	multi	multiphase
anti	antisocial	non	nonsignificant
bi	bilingual	over	overaggressive
cede	intercede	phobia	agoraphobia
co	coworker	post	posttest
counter	counterbalance	pre	preexperimental
equi	equimax	pro	prowar
extra	extracurricular	pseudo	pseudoscience
gram	cardiogram	quasi	quasiperiodic
infra	infrared	re	reevaluate
inter	interstimulus	semi	semidarkness
intra	intraspecific	socio	socioeconomic
like	wavelike	sub	subtest
macro	macrocosm	super	superordinate
mega	megawatt	supra	supraliminal
meta	metacognitive	ultra	ultrahigh
meter	micrometer	un	unbiased
micro	microcosm	under	underdeveloped
mid	midterm		

Exceptions: Use a hyphen in *meta-analysis* and *quasi-experimental.*

modify *lists*, thus, *different-word lists*). Likewise, "the adolescents resided in two parent homes" means that two homes served as residences, whereas if the adolescents resided in "two-parent homes," they each would live in a household headed by two parents. A properly placed hyphen helps the reader understand the intended meaning.

Table 2.3. Prefixed Words That Require Hyphens

Occurrence	Example
1. Compounds in which the base word is capitalized a number an abbreviation more than one word	■ pro-Freudian ■ post-1970 ■ pre-UCS trial ■ non-achievement-oriented students
2. All *self-* compounds, whether they are adjectives or nouns[a]	■ self-report technique ■ the test was self-paced ■ self-esteem
3. Words that could be misunderstood	■ re-pair [pair again] ■ re-form [form again] ■ un-ionized
4. Words in which the prefix ends and the base word begins with the same vowel[b]	■ meta-analysis ■ anti-intellectual ■ co-occur

[a]But *self psychology.* [b]*Pre* and *re* compounds are usually set solid to base words beginning with *e.*

General Principle 3

Most compound adjective rules are applicable only when the compound adjective precedes the term it modifies. If a compound adjective follows the term, do not use a hyphen, because relationships are sufficiently clear without one. The following examples are all correctly hyphenated:

> client-centered counseling

but

> the counseling was client centered

> *t*-test results

but

> results from *t* tests

same-sex children

but

children of the same sex

General Principle 4

Write most words formed with prefixes as one word (see Table 2.2). Table 2.3 contains some exceptions.

General Principle 5

When two or more compound modifiers have a common base, that base is sometimes omitted in all except the last modifier, but the hyphens are retained.

long- and short-term memory

2-, 3-, and 10-min trials

Capitalization

Use an uppercase letter for the first letter of a word according to the guidelines in the following sections.

2.15 Words Beginning a Sentence

Capitalize

■ the first word in a complete sentence.

Note: If a name that begins with a lowercase letter begins a sentence, then it should be capitalized. Do not begin a sentence with a statistical term (e.g., *t* test or *p* value; see section 3.11 for abbreviations beginning a sentence).

Correct:

De Waal (1994) concluded the following

Incorrect:

de Waal (1994) concluded the following

- the first word after a colon that begins a complete sentence.

> The author made one main point: No explanation that has been suggested so far answers all questions.

2.16 Major Words in Titles and Headings

Capitalize

- major words in titles of books and articles within the body of the paper. Conjunctions, articles, and short prepositions are not considered major words; however, capitalize all words of four letters or more. Capitalize all verbs (including linking verbs), nouns, adjectives, adverbs, and pronouns. When a capitalized word is a hyphenated compound, capitalize both words. Also, capitalize the first word after a colon or a dash in a title.

> In her book, *History of Pathology*

> The criticism of the article, "Attitudes Toward Mental Health Workers"

> "Memory in Hearing-Impaired Children: Implications for Vocabulary Development"

Exception: In titles of books and articles in reference lists, capitalize only the first word, the first word after a colon or em dash, and proper nouns. Do not capitalize the second word of a hyphenated compound. (See Chapter 7 for further discussion of reference style.)

> Liu, D., Wellman, H. M., Tardif, T., & Sabbagh, M. A. (2008). Theory of mind development in Chinese children: A meta-analysis of false-belief understanding across cultures and languages. *Developmental Psychology, 44,* 523–531. doi:10.1037/0012-1649.44.2.523

- major words in article headings and subheadings.

Exception: In indented paragraph (Levels 3, 4, and 5) headings, capitalize only the first word and proper nouns (see section 1.03).

- major words in table titles and figure legends. In table headings and figure captions, capitalize only the first word and proper nouns (see sections 5.13 for table headings and 5.23 for figure captions).
- references to titles of sections within the same article.

    as explained in the Method section

    which is discussed in the Data Analyses subsection

2.17 Proper Nouns and Trade Names

Capitalize

- proper nouns and adjectives and words used as proper nouns. Proper adjectives that have acquired a common meaning are not capitalized; consult *Merriam-Webster's Collegiate Dictionary* (2005) for guidance.

    Freudian slip

    Wilks's lambda

    Greco-Latin square

    but

    eustachian tube

    cesarean section

- names of university departments if they refer to a specific department within a specific university and complete names of academic courses if they refer to a specific course.

    Department of Sociology, University of Washington

Psychology 101

Developmental Psychopathology

but

a sociology department

an introductory psychology course

■ trade and brand names of drugs, equipment, and food.

Elavil [*but* amitriptyline hydrochloride]

Hunter Klockounter

Plexiglas

Purina Monkey Chow

Xerox

Do not capitalize names of laws, theories, models, statistical procedures, or hypotheses.

the empirical law of effect

parallel distributed processing model

associative learning model

a two-group *t* test

but

Gregory's theory of illusions [Retain uppercase in personal names.]

Fisher's *r* to *Z* transformation

2.18 Nouns Followed by Numerals or Letters

Capitalize nouns followed by numerals or letters that denote a specific place in a numbered series.

On Day 2 of Experiment 4

during Trial 5, the no-delay group performed

as shown in Table 2, Figure 3B, and Chapter 4

Grant AG02726 from the National Institute on Aging

Exception: Do not capitalize nouns that denote common parts of books or tables followed by numerals or letters.

page iv

row 3

column 5

Do not capitalize nouns that precede a variable.

trial *n* and item *x*

but

Trial 3 and Item b [The number and letter are not variables.]

2.19 Titles of Tests

Capitalize exact, complete titles of published and unpublished tests. Words such as *test* or *scale* are not capitalized if they refer to subscales of tests.

Minnesota Multiphasic Personality Inventory

Stroop Color–Word Interference Test

but

MMPI Depression scale

Do not capitalize shortened, inexact, or generic titles of tests.

a vocabulary test   Stroop color test

2.20 Names of Conditions or Groups in an Experiment

Do not capitalize names of conditions or groups in an experiment.

experimental and control groups

participants were assigned to information and no-information conditions

but

Conditions A and B [See section 2.18.]

2.21 Names of Factors, Variables, and Effects

Capitalize names of derived variables within a factor or principal components analysis. The words *factor* and *component* are not capitalized unless followed by a number (see section 2.18).

Mealtime Behavior (Factor 4)

Component 1

Do not capitalize effects or variables unless they appear with multiplication signs. (Take care that you do not use the term *factor* when you mean *effect* or *variable*, for example, in an interaction or analysis of variance.)

a small age effect

the sex, age, and weight variables

but

the Sex × Age × Weight interaction

a 3 × 3 × 2 (Groups × Trials × Responses) design

a 2 (methods) × 2 (item types)

Italicizing and Abbreviating

This chapter provides guidelines on the use of italics and abbreviations in scientific writing. We outline APA Style requirements, provide examples, and offer lists of Latin abbreviations and common abbreviations for units of measurement.

Italics

In general, use italics infrequently.

3.01 Correct Use of Italics

Use italics for

- titles of books, periodicals, films, videos, TV shows, and microfilm publications.

  The Elements of Style

  American Psychologist

Exception: Words within the title of a book in text that would normally be italicized should be set in Roman type (this is referred to as *reverse italicization*).

A Stereotaxic Atlas of the Monkey Brain (Macaca Mulatta)

Dreaming by the Book: Freud's The Interpretation of Dreams *and the History of the Psychoanalytic Movement*

■ genera, species, and varieties.

Macaca mulatta

■ introduction of a new, technical, or key term or label (after a term has been used once, do not italicize it).

The term *backward masking*

box labeled *empty*

■ a letter, word, or phrase cited as a linguistic example.

words such as *big* and *little*

the letter *a*

the meaning of *to fit tightly together*

a row of *X*s

■ words that could be misread.

the *small* group [meaning a designation, not group size]

■ letters used as statistical symbols or algebraic variables.

Cohen's $d = 0.084$

$a/b = c/d$

SEM

■ some test scores and scales.

Rorschach scores: *F*+%, *Z*

MMPI scales: *Hs, Pd*

- periodical volume numbers in reference lists.

    American Psychologist, 26, 46–67

- anchors of a scale.

    health ratings ranged from 1 (*poor*) to 5 (*excellent*)

3.02 Incorrect Use of Italics

Do not use italics for

- foreign phrases and abbreviations common in English (i.e., phrases found as main entries in *Merriam-Webster's Collegiate Dictionary*, 2005).

    a posteriori   et al.

    a priori   per se

- chemical terms.

    NaCl, LSD

- trigonometric terms.

    sin, tan, log

- nonstatistical subscripts to statistical symbols or mathematical expressions.

    F_{max}

    $S_A + S_B$

- Greek letters.

    β

- mere emphasis. (Italics are acceptable if emphasis might otherwise be lost; in general, however, use syntax to provide emphasis.)

Incorrect:

> it is *important* to bear in mind that *this* process is *not* proposed as a *stage* theory of developments.

■ letters used as abbreviations.

> intertrial interval (ITI)

Abbreviations
3.03 Use of Abbreviations

To maximize clarity, use abbreviations sparingly. Although abbreviations are sometimes useful for long, technical terms in scientific writing, communication is usually garbled rather than clarified if, for example, an abbreviation is unfamiliar to the reader.

Overuse. Consider whether the space saved by abbreviations in the following sentence justifies the time necessary to master the meaning:

> The advantage of the LH was clear from the RT data, which reflected high FP and FN rates for the RH.

Without abbreviations the passage reads as follows:

> The advantage of the left hand was clear from the reaction time data, which reflected high false-positive and false-negative rates for the right hand.

Underuse. Abbreviations introduced on first mention of a term and used fewer than three times thereafter, particularly in a long paper, may be difficult for a reader to remember, and you probably serve the reader best if you write them out each time. In the following example, however, a standard abbreviation for a long, familiar term eases the reader's task:

> Patients at seven hospitals completed the MMPI–2.

Deciding whether to abbreviate. In all circumstances other than in the reference list (see section 7.23) and in the abstract, you must decide whether (a) to spell out a given expression every time it is used in an article or (b) to spell it out initially and abbreviate it thereafter. For example, the abbreviations *L* for large and *S* for small in a paper discussing different sequences of reward (*LLSS* or *LSLS*) would be an effective and readily understood shortcut. In another paper, however, writing about the *L reward* and the *S reward* would be both unnecessary and confusing. In most instances, abbreviating experimental group names is ineffective because the abbreviations are not adequately informative or easily recognizable and may even be more cumbersome than the full name. In general, use an abbreviation only (a) if it is conventional and if the reader is more familiar with the abbreviation than with the complete form or (b) if considerable space can be saved and cumbersome repetition avoided. In short, use only those abbreviations that will help you communicate with your readers. Remember, they have not had the same experience with your abbreviations as you have.

3.04 Explanation of Abbreviations

Because the abbreviations that psychologists use in their daily writing may not be familiar to students or to readers in other disciplines or other countries, a term to be abbreviated must, on its first appearance, be written out completely and followed immediately by its abbreviation in parentheses. Thereafter, use the abbreviation in text without further explanation (do not switch between the abbreviated and written-out forms of a term).

> The results of studies of simple reaction time (RT) to a visual target have shown a strong negative relation between RT and luminance.

Explain abbreviations that appear in a figure in the caption or legend. Explain those that appear in a table either in the table title (if it includes words that are abbreviated in the table body; see section 5.12) or in the table note (see section 5.16). Explain an abbreviation that is used in several figures or tables in each figure or table in which the abbreviation is used. Avoid introducing abbreviations into figure captions or table notes if they do not appear in the figure or table. Standard abbreviations for units of measurement do not need to be written out on first use (see section 3.08).

3.05 Abbreviations Accepted as Words

APA Style permits the use of abbreviations that appear as word entries (i.e., that are not labeled *abbr*) in *Merriam-Webster's Collegiate Dictionary* (2005). Such abbreviations do not need explanation in text.

> IQ   REM   ESP   AIDS   HIV   NADP   ACTH

3.06 Abbreviations Used Often in APA Journals

Some abbreviations may not be in the dictionary but appear frequently in the journal for which you are writing. Although probably well understood by many readers, these abbreviations should still be explained when first used.

> Minnesota Multiphasic Personality Inventory (MMPI)
>
> conditional stimulus (CS)
>
> intertrial interval (ITI)
>
> consonant–vowel–consonant (CVC)
>
> short-term memory (STM)
>
> reaction time (RT)

Do not use the abbreviations *S*, *E*, or *O* for subject, experimenter, and observer.

3.07 Latin Abbreviations

Use the following standard Latin abbreviations only in parenthetical material; in nonparenthetical material, use the English translation of the Latin terms; in both cases, include the correct punctuation that accompanies the term:

cf.	compare	i.e.,	that is,
e.g.,	for example,	viz.,	namely,
, etc.	, and so forth	vs.	versus, against

Exception: Use the abbreviation *v.* (for *versus*) in references and text citations to court cases, whether parenthetical or not (see Appendix 8.1, section A8.03, Examples 1–8).

Exception: In the reference list and in text, use the Latin abbreviation *et al.,* which means *and others*, in nonparenthetical as well as parenthetical material.

3.08 Scientific Abbreviations

Units of measurement. Use abbreviations and symbols for metric and nonmetric units of measurement that are accompanied by numeric values (e.g., 4 cm, 30 s, 12 min, 18 hr, 45°). (See Table 3.1 for a list of some common abbreviations used for units of measurement.)

Do not repeat abbreviated units of measure when expressing multiple amounts:

    16–30 kHz   0.3, 1.5, and 3.0 mg/dl

Write out abbreviations for units that are not accompanied by numeric values (e.g., measured in centimeters, several kilograms).

Units of time. To prevent misreading, do not abbreviate the following units of time, even when they are accompanied by numeric values:

    day   week   month   year

Table 3.1. Common Abbreviations for Units of Measurement

Abbreviation	Unit of measurement
A	ampere
Å	angstrom
AC	alternating current
a.m.	ante meridiem
°C	degree Celsius
Ci	curie
cm	centimeter
cps	cycles per second
dB	decibel (specify scale)
DC	direct current
deg/s	degrees per second
dl	deciliter
°F	degree Fahrenheit
g	gram
g	gravity
Hz	hertz
in.	inch (include metric equivalent in parentheses)
IQ	intelligence quotient
IU	international unit
kg	kilogram
km	kilometer
kph	kilometers per hour
kW	kilowatt
L	liter
m	meter
μm	micrometer
mA	milliampere

Table 3.1. Common Abbreviations for Units of Measurement (continued)

Abbreviation	Unit of measurement
mEq	milliequivalent
meV	million electron volts
mg	milligram
ml	milliliter
mm	millimeter
mM	millimolar
mmHg	millimeters of mercury
mmol	millimole
mol wt	molecular weight
mph	miles per hour (include metric equivalent in parentheses)
$M\Omega$	megohm
N	newton
p.m.	post meridiem
ppm	parts per million
psi	pounds per square inch (include metric equivalent in parentheses)
rpm	revolutions per minute
S	Siemens
V	volt
W	watt

Abbreviate the following units of time:

> hr, hour
>
> min, minute
>
> ms, millisecond
>
> ns, nanosecond
>
> s, second

Chemical compounds. Chemical compounds may be expressed by common name or by chemical name. If you prefer to use the common name, provide the chemical name in parentheses on first mention in the Method section. Avoid expressing compounds with chemical formulas, as these are usually less informative to the reader and have a high likelihood of being typed or typeset incorrectly (e.g., aspirin or salicylic acid, *not* $C_9H_8O_4$). If names of compounds include Greek letters, retain the letters as symbols and do not write them out (e.g., β carotene, *not* beta carotene).

Long names of organic compounds are often abbreviated; if the abbreviation is listed as a word entry in *Merriam-Webster's Collegiate Dictionary* (2005; e.g., NADP for *nicotinamide adenine dinucleotide phosphate*), you may use it freely, without writing it out on first use.

Concentrations. If you express a solution as a percentage concentration instead of as a molar concentration, be sure to specify the percentage as a weight-per-volume ratio (wt/vol), a volume ratio (vol/vol), or a weight ratio (wt/wt) of solute to solvent. The higher the concentration is, the more ambiguous the expression as a percentage. Specifying the ratio is especially necessary for concentrations of alcohol, glucose, and sucrose. Specifying the salt form is also essential for precise reporting: *d*-amphetamine HCl or *d*-amphetamine SO_4 (note that expression of chemical name in combination with a formula is acceptable in this case).

> 12% (vol/vol) ethyl alcohol solution
>
> 1% (wt/vol) saccharin solution

Routes of administration. You may abbreviate a route of administration when it is paired with a number-and-unit combination. Preferred style for APA is no periods: icv = intracerebral ventricular, im = intramuscular, ip = intraperitoneal, iv = intravenous, sc = subcutaneous, and so forth.

anesthetized with sodium pentobarbital
(90 mg/kg ip)

but

the first of two subcutaneous injections (*not* sc
injections)

3.09 Other Abbreviations

Use abbreviations for statistics as described in section
4.15. For information on the International System of
Units (SI), see the APA Style website (www.apastyle.org).

3.10 Plurals of Abbreviations

To form the plural of most abbreviations and statistical
symbols, add *s* alone, but not italicized and without an
apostrophe.

IQs   Eds.   vols.   *M*s   *p*s   *n*s

Exception: Do not add an *s* to make abbreviations of units
of measurement plural (e.g., 12 cm; see section 3.08).

Exception: To form the plural of the reference abbreviation *p.* (page), write pp.; do not add an *s*.

3.11 Abbreviations Beginning a
Sentence

Never begin a sentence with a lowercase abbreviation
(e.g., lb) or a symbol that stands alone (e.g., α). Begin a
sentence with a capitalized abbreviation or acronym
(e.g., U.S. or APA) or with a symbol connected to a word
(e.g., β-Endorphins) only when necessary to avoid indi-
rect and awkward writing. In the case of chemical compounds, capitalize the first letter of the word to which the
symbol is connected; keep the locant, descriptor, or po-
sitional prefix (i.e., Greek, small capital, and italic letters
and numerals) intact.

In running text:	*At beginning of sentence:*
L-methionine	L-Methionine
N,*N*'-dimethylurea	*N*,*N*'-Dimethylurea
γ-hydroxy-β-aminobutyric acid	γ-Hydroxy-β-aminobutyric acid

4

Numbers, Metrication, and Statistics

This chapter describes the style for presenting numbers, metrication, and statistics in scientific writing. The sections present rules, exceptions, and special usages of numbers; recommendations on using the metric system in journals; and guidelines on presenting statistical and mathematical copy.

Numbers

The general rule governing APA Style on the use of numbers is to use numerals to express numbers 10 and above and words to express numbers below 10. Sections 4.01–4.04 expand on this rule and state exceptions and special usages.

4.01 Numbers Expressed in Numerals

Use numerals to express

a. numbers 10 and above. (*Exceptions:* See sections 4.03–4.04.)

12 cm wide	10th-grade students
the remaining 10%	13 lists
25 years old	105 stimulus words

b. numbers in the abstract of a paper or in a graphical display within a paper.

c. numbers that immediately precede a unit of measurement.

a 5-mg dose

with 10.54 cm of

d. numbers that represent statistical or mathematical functions, fractional or decimal quantities, percentages, ratios, and percentiles and quartiles.

multiplied by 5

3 times as many [proportion]

0.33 of the

more than 5% of the sample

a ratio of 16:1

the 5th percentile

e. numbers that represent time, dates, ages, scores and points on a scale, exact sums of money, and numerals as numerals.

1 hr 34 min

at 12:30 a.m.

2-year-olds

scored 4 on a 7-point scale

Exception: Use words for approximations of numbers of days, months, and years (e.g., about three months ago).

f. numbers that denote a specific place in a numbered series, parts of books and tables, and each number in a list of four or more numbers.

> Grade 8 [*but* the eighth grade; see section 4.04]
>
> Table 3
>
> row 5

4.02 Numbers Expressed in Words

Use words to express

a. any number that begins a sentence, title, or text heading. (Whenever possible, reword the sentence to avoid beginning with a number.)

> Forty-eight percent of the sample showed an increase; 2% showed no change.
>
> Twelve students improved, and 12 students did not improve.

b. common fractions

> one fifth of the class
>
> two-thirds majority

c. universally accepted usage

> the Twelve Apostles
>
> Five Pillars of Islam

4.03 Combining Numerals and Words to Express Numbers

Use a combination of numerals and words to express back-to-back modifiers.

> 2 two-way interactions
>
> ten 7-point scales

A combination of numerals and words in these situations increases the clarity and readability of the construction. In some situations, however, readability may suffer; in such a case, spell out both numbers.

Correct:

first two items

Incorrect:

1st two items

first 2 items

4.04 Ordinal Numbers

Treat ordinal numbers as you would cardinal numbers (see sections 4.01–4.03).

Ordinal	Cardinal base
second-order factor	two orders
the fourth graders	four grades
the first item of the 75th trial	one item, 75 trials
the 2nd and 11th rows	2 rows, 11 rows

4.05 Decimal Fractions

Use a zero before the decimal point with numbers that are less than 1 when the statistic can exceed 1.

0.23 cm

Cohen's $d = 0.70$

0.48 s

Do not use a zero before a decimal fraction when the statistic cannot be greater than 1 (e.g., correlations, proportions, and levels of statistical significance).

$r(24) = -.43, p = .028$

The number of decimal places to use in reporting the results of experiments and data analytic manipulations of the data should be governed by the following general principle: Round as much as possible while keeping prospective use and statistical precision in mind. As a general rule, fewer decimal digits are easier to comprehend than more digits; therefore, in general, it is better to round to two decimal places or to rescale the measurement (in which case effect sizes should be presented in the same metric). For instance, a difference in distances that must be carried to four decimals to be seen when scaled in meters can be more effectively illustrated in millimeters, which would require only a few decimal digits to illustrate the same difference. As a rule, when properly scaled, most data can be effectively presented with two decimal digits of accuracy. Report correlations, proportions, and inferential statistics such as t, F, and χ^2 to two decimals.

When reporting p values, report exact p values (e.g., $p = .031$) to two or three decimal places. However, report p values less than .001 as $p < .001$. The tradition of reporting p values in the form $p < .10$, $p < .05$, $p < .01$, and so forth, was appropriate in a time when only limited tables of critical values were available. However, in tables the "$p <$" notation may be necessary for clarity (see section 5.16).

4.06 Roman Numerals

If Roman numerals are part of an established terminology, do not change to Arabic numerals; for example, use Type II error. Use Arabic, not Roman, numerals for routine seriation (e.g., Step 1).

4.07 Commas in Numbers

Use commas between groups of three digits in most figures of 1,000 or more.

Exceptions:

page numbers	page 1029
binary digits	00110010
serial numbers	290466960
degrees of temperature	3071 °F
acoustic frequency designations	2000 Hz
degrees of freedom	$F(24, 1000)$

4.08 Plurals of Numbers

To form the plurals of numbers, whether expressed as figures or as words, add *s* or *es* alone, without an apostrophe.

fours and sixes   1950s   10s and 20s

Metrication
4.09 Policy on Metrication

APA uses the metric system in its journals. All references to physical measurements, where feasible, should be expressed in metric units. The metric system outlined in this section is based, with some exceptions, on the International System of Units (SI), which is an extension and refinement of the traditional metric system and is supported by the national standardizing bodies in many countries, including the United States.

In preparing manuscripts, use metric units if possible. If you use instruments that record measurements in nonmetric units, you may report the nonmetric units but also report the established SI equivalents in parentheses immediately after the nonmetric units.

The rods were spaced 19 mm apart. [Measurement was made in metric units.]

The rod was 3 ft (0.91 m) long. [Measurement was made in nonmetric units and converted to the rounded SI equivalent.]

4.10 Style for Metric Units

Abbreviation. Use the metric symbol (see International System [SI] Base and Supplementary Units and other resources on metrication at www.apastyle.org) to express a metric unit when it appears with a numeric value (e.g., 4 m). When a metric unit does not appear with a numeric value, spell out the unit in text (e.g., measured in meters) and use the metric symbol in column and headings of tables to conserve space (e.g., lag in ms).

Capitalization. Use lowercase letters when writing out full names of units (e.g., meter, nanometer), unless the name appears in capitalized material or at the beginning of a sentence.

For the most part, use lowercase letters for symbols (e.g., cd), even in capitalized material. Symbols derived from the name of a person usually include uppercase letters (e.g., Gy), as do symbols for some prefixes that represent powers of 10: exa (E), peta (P), tera (T), giga (G), and mega (M). (See Table 3.1, pp. 80–81 for more examples.)

Use the symbol *L* for liter when it stands alone (e.g., 5 L, 0.3 mg/L) because a lowercase *l* may be misread as the numeral one (use lowercase *l* for fractions of a liter: 5 ml, 9 ng/dl).

Plurals. Make full names of units plural when appropriate.

meters

Do not make symbols or abbreviations of units plural.

3 cm, *not* 3 cms

Periods. Do not use a period after a symbol, except at the end of a sentence.

Spacing. Use a space between a symbol and the number to which it refers, except for measures of angles (e.g., degrees, minutes, and seconds).

4.5 m, 12 °C, but 45° angle

Compound units. Use a centered dot between the symbols of a compound term formed by the multiplication of units.

Pa • s

Use a space between full names of units of a compound unit formed by the multiplication of units; do not use a centered dot.

pascal second

Statistical and Mathematical Copy

APA Style for presenting statistical and mathematical copy reflects (a) standards of content and form agreed on in the field and (b) the requirements of clear communication.

4.11 Selecting Effective Presentation

Statistical and mathematical copy can be presented in text, in tables, and in figures. Detailed discussions of principles for the generation of tables, figures, and graphs can be found in Chapter 5. In deciding which approach to take, a general rule that might prove useful is

- if you need to present three or fewer numbers, first try using a sentence;
- if you need to present four to 20 numbers, first consider using a well-prepared table; and
- if you have more than 20 numbers, a graph is often more useful than a table.

Select the mode of presentation that optimizes understanding of the data by the reader. Detailed displays that allow fine-grained understanding of a data set may be more appropriate to include in online supplemental archives (for more information about online supplemental archives, see section 6.04) than in the print version of an article. Tables, figures, charts, and other graphics should be prepared with the understanding that if the manuscript is accepted, they are to be published at the editor's discretion. In any case, be prepared to submit tables and figures of complex statistical and mathematical material if an editor requests them.

4.12 References for Statistics

Do not give a reference for statistics in common use; this convention applies to most statistics used in journal articles. Do give a reference when (a) less common statistics are used, especially those that have appeared so recently that they can be found only in journals; (b) a statistic is used in an unconventional or a controversial way; or (c) the statistic itself is the focus of the article.

4.13 Formulas

Do not give a formula for a statistic in common use; do give a formula when the statistic or mathematical expression is new, rare, or essential to the manuscript. Presentation of equations is described in sections 4.17–4.18.

4.14 Statistics in Text

When reporting inferential statistics (e.g., t tests, F tests, χ^2 tests, and associated effect sizes and confidence intervals), include sufficient information to allow the reader to fully understand the analyses conducted. The data supplied, preferably in the text but possibly in an online supplemental archive depending on the magnitude of such data arrays, should allow the reader to confirm the basic reported analyses (e.g., cell means, standard deviations, sample sizes, and correlations) and should enable the interested reader to construct some effect-size estimates and confidence intervals beyond those supplied in the paper per se. In the case of multilevel data, present summary statistics for each level of aggregation. What constitutes sufficient information depends on the analytic approach reported.

For immediate recognition, the omnibus test of the main effect of sentence format was statistically significant, $F(2, 177) = 6.30$, $p = .002$, est $\omega^2 = .07$. The one-degree-of-freedom contrast of primary interest (the mean difference between Conditions 1 and 2) was also statistically significant at the specified .05 level, $t(177) = 3.51$, $p < .001$, $d = 0.65$, 95% CI [0.35, 0.95].

High-school GPA statistically predicted college mathematics performance, $R^2 = .12$, $F(1, 148) = 20.18$, $p < .001$, 95% CI [.02, .22]. The four-subtest battery added to this prediction, $R^2 = .21$, $\Delta R^2 = .09$, $F(4, 144) = 3.56$, $p = .004$, 95% CI [.10, .32]. Most important, when the two preceding variables were statistically accounted for, the college mathematics placement examination also explained unique variance in students' college mathematics performance, $R^2 = .25$, $\Delta R^2 = .04$, $F(1, 143) = 7.63$, $p = .006$, 95% CI [.13, .37].

If you present descriptive statistics in a table or figure, you do not need to repeat them in text, although you should (a) mention the table in which the statistics can be found and (b) emphasize particular data in the narrative when they help in interpretation of the findings.

When enumerating a series of similar statistics, be certain that the relation between the statistics and their referents is clear. Words such as *respectively* and *in order* can clarify this relationship.

Means (with standard deviations in parentheses) for Trials 1 through 4 were 2.43 (0.50), 2.59 (1.21), 2.68 (0.39), and 2.86 (0.12), respectively.

When reporting confidence intervals, use the format 95% CI [LL, UL], where LL is the lower limit of the confidence interval and UL is the upper limit.

When a sequence of confidence intervals is repeated in a series or within the same paragraph and the level of confidence (e.g., 95%) has remained unchanged, and the meaning is clear, you do not need to repeat the 95% CI. Every report of a confidence interval must clearly state the level of confidence. A sentence might then read, in part,

> 95% CIs [5.62, 8.31], [−2.43, 4.31], and [−4.29, −3.11], respectively

When a confidence interval follows reporting of a point estimate, the units of measurement should not be repeated:

> M = 30.5 cm, 99% CI [18.0, 43.0]

4.15 Statistical Symbols

When using a statistical term in the narrative, use the term, not the symbol. For example, use

> The means were

not

> The Ms were

Symbols for population versus sample statistics. Population parameters are usually represented by Greek letters. Most estimators are represented by italicized Latin letters. For example, the population correlation would be represented as ρ, and the estimator would be represented as r. [Est(ρ) and $\hat{\rho}$ are also acceptable]. Some test statistics are represented by italicized Latin letters (e.g., t and F), and a few are represented by Greek letters (e.g., Γ).

Symbols for number of subjects. Use an uppercase, italicized N to designate the number of members in the total sample (e.g., N = 135) and a lowercase, italicized n to designate the number of members in a limited portion of the total sample (e.g., n = 30).

Symbol for percentage. Use the symbol for percent only when it is preceded by a numeral. Use the word *percentage* when a number is not given.

> found that 18% of the rats

> determined the percentage of rats

Exception: In table headings and figure legends, use the symbol % to conserve space.

Standard, boldface, and italic type. Statistical symbols and mathematical copy in manuscripts are prepared with three different typefaces: standard, **boldface**, and *italic*. The same typeface is used in text, tables, and figures.

Greek letters, subscripts, and superscripts that function as identifiers (i.e., are not variables) and abbreviations that are not variables (e.g., log, GLM, WLS) are set in standard typeface.

μ_{girls}, α, β_i

Symbols for vectors and matrices are set in boldface.

$\mathbf{V}$, $\mathbf{\Sigma}$

All other statistical symbols are set in italic type.

N, M_x, df, SSE, MSE, t, F

On occasion, an element may serve as both an abbreviation and a symbol (e.g., *SD*); in those cases, use the typeface that reflects the function of element (see Table 4.1).

Identifying letters and symbols. As with all aspects of manuscript preparation, take care to ensure that there are no ambiguities that could lead to errors in the final production steps, particularly with mathematical and statistical symbols, non-English characters, and complex alignments (e.g., subscripts and superscripts). Avoid misunderstandings and corrections by preparing mathematical copy carefully.

Table 4.1. Statistical Abbreviations and Symbols

Abbreviation/symbol	Definition
English character set	
a	In item response theory, the slope parameter
AIC	Akaike information criterion
ANCOVA	Analysis of covariance
ANOVA	Analysis of variance
b, b_i	In regression and multiple regression analyses, estimated values of raw (unstandardized) regression coefficients; in item response theory, the difficulty-severity parameter
b^*, b_i^*	Estimated values of standardized regression coefficients in regression and multiple regression analyses
BIC	Bayesian information criterion
CAT	Computerized adaptive testing
CDF	Cumulative distribution function
CFA	Confirmatory factor analysis
CI	Confidence interval
d	Cohen's measure of sample effect size for comparing two sample means
d'	Discriminability, a measure of sensitivity in signal detection theory
df	Degrees of freedom
DIF	Differential item functioning
EFA	Exploratory factor analysis
EM	Expectation maximization
ES	Effect size
f	Frequency
f_e	Expected frequency

Table 4.1. Statistical Abbreviations and Symbols (continued)

Abbreviation/ symbol	Definition
f_o	Observed frequency
F	F distribution, Fisher's F ratio
$F(v_1, v_2)$	F with v_1 and v_2 degrees of freedom
F_{crit}	Critical value for statistical significance in an F test
F_{max}	Hartley's test of homogeneity of variance
FIML	Full information maximum likelihood
g	Hedges's measure of effect size
GLM	Generalized linear model
GLS	Generalized least squares
H_0	Null hypothesis, hypothesis under test
H_1 (or H_a)	Alternative hypothesis
HLM	Hierarchical linear model(ing)
HSD	Tukey's honestly significant difference
IRT	Item response theory
k	Coefficient of alienation; number of studies in a meta-analysis; number of levels in an experimental design or individual study
k^2	Coefficient of nondetermination
KR20	Kuder–Richardson reliability index
LGC	Latent growth curve
LL	Lower limit (as of a CI)
LR	Likelihood ratio
LSD	Least significant difference
M (or $\bar{X}$)	Sample mean, arithmetic average
MANOVA	Multivariate analysis of variance
MANCOVA	Multivariate analysis of covariance
MCMC	Markov chain Monte Carlo

Table 4.1. Statistical Abbreviations and Symbols
(continued)

Abbreviation/ symbol	Definition
Mdn	Median
MLE	Maximum likelihood estimator, maximum likelihood estimate
MS	Mean square
MSE	Mean square error
n	Number of cases (generally in a subsample)
N	Total number of cases
ns	Not statistically significant
OLS	Ordinary least squares
OR	Odds ratio
p	Probability; probability of a success in a binary trial
p_{rep}	The probability a replication would give a result with the same sign as the original result
PDF	Probability density function
q	Probability of a failure in a binary trial, $1 - p$
Q	Test of homogeneity of effect sizes
r	Estimate of the Pearson product–moment correlation coefficient
$r_{ab.c}$	The partial correlation of a and b with the effect of c removed
$r_{a(b.c)}$	The part (or semipartial) correlation of a and b with the effect of c removed from b
r^2	Coefficient of determination; measure of strength of relationship; estimate of the Pearson product–moment correlation squared
r_b	Biserial correlation
r_{pb}	Point biserial correlation

Table 4.1. Statistical Abbreviations and Symbols
(continued)

Abbreviation/symbol	Definition
r_s	Spearman rank order correlation
R	Multiple correlation
R^2	Multiple correlation squared; measure of strength of association
RMSEA	Root mean square error of approximation
s	Sample standard deviation (denominator $\sqrt{n-1}$)
S	Sample variance–covariance matrix
S^2	Sample variance (biased estimator) – denominator n
s^2	Sample variance (unbiased) – denominator $n-1$
SD	Standard deviation
SE	Standard error
SEM	Standard error of measurement; standard error of the mean
SEM	Structural equation modeling
SS	Sum of squares
t	Student's t distribution; a statistical test based on the Student t distribution; the sample value of the t-test statistic
T_k	Generic effect size estimate
T^2	Hotelling's multivariate test for the equality of the mean vector in two multivariate populations
U	The Mann–Whitney test statistic
UL	Upper limit (as of a CI)
V	Pillai–Bartlett multivariate trace criterion; Cramér's measure of association in contingency tables
w_k	Fixed effects weights
w_{k*}	Random effects weights

Table 4.1. Statistical Abbreviations and Symbols (continued)

Abbreviation/ symbol	Definition
W	Kendall's coefficient of concordance and its estimate
WLS	Weighted least squares
z	A standardized score; the value of a statistic divided by its standard error
Greek character set	
α	In statistical hypothesis testing, the probability of making a Type I error; Cronbach's index of internal consistency (a form of reliability)
β	In statistical hypothesis testing, the probability of making a Type II error ($1 - \beta$, denotes statistical power); population values of regression coefficients (with appropriate subscripts as needed)
Γ	Goodman–Kruskal's index of relationship
δ	Population value of Cohen's effect size; noncentrality parameter in hypothesis testing and noncentral distributions
ε^2	Measure of strength of relationship in analysis of variance
Δ	Increment of change
η^2	Measure of strength of relationship (eta squared)
θ_k	Generic effect size in meta analysis
Θ	Roy's multivariate test criterion
κ	Cohen's measure of agreement corrected for chance agreement
λ	Element of a factor loading matrix
λ	Goodman–Kruskal measure of predictability
Λ	Wilks's multivariate test criterion
μ	Population mean; expected value
ν	Degrees of freedom

Table 4.1. Statistical Abbreviations and Symbols (continued)

Abbreviation/ symbol	Definition
ρ	Population product–moment correlation
ρ_I	Population intraclass correlation
σ	Population standard deviation
σ^2	Population variance
Σ	Population variance–covariance matrix
τ	Kendall's rank-order correlation coefficient; Hotelling's multivariate trace criterion
ϕ	Standard normal probability density function
Φ	Measure of association in contingency tables; standard normal cumulative distribution function
χ^2	The chi-square distribution; a statistical test based on the chi-square distribution; the sample value of the chi-square test statistic
Ψ	In statistical hypothesis testing, a statistical contrast
ω^2	Strength of a statistical relationship
Mathematical symbols	
$\lvert a \rvert$	Absolute value of a
Σ	Summation

Note. Some forms are used as both abbreviations and symbols. Use the abbreviation form when referring to the concept and the symbol form when specifying a numeric value. As a rule, the symbol form will be either a non-English letter or an italicized version of the English letter form. Most abbreviations can be turned into symbols (for use when reporting numerical estimates) by simply italicizing the abbreviation. In addition, it is acceptable to use the form est(θ) or $\hat{\theta}$ to indicate an estimator or estimate of the parameter θ.

4.16 Spacing, Alignment, and Punctuation

Space mathematical copy as you would space words: $a+b=c$ is as difficult to read as *wordswithoutspacing*. Instead, type $a + b = c$.

Align signs and symbols carefully. Use the subscript and superscript features in your word-processing software. In most cases, type subscripts first and then superscripts (x_a^2). However, place a superscript such as the symbol for prime right next to its letter or symbol (x'_a). Because APA prefers to align subscripts and superscripts one under the other (*stacking*) for ease of reading instead of setting one to the right of the other (*staggering*), that is how they are normally typeset. If subscripts and superscripts should not be stacked, so indicate in a cover letter or on the manuscript.

Equations

Punctuate all equations, whether they are in the line of text or displayed (i.e., typed on a new line), to conform to their place in the syntax of the sentence (see the period following Equation 3 in section 4.18). If an equation exceeds the column width of a typeset page (approximately 55 characters, including spaces, will fit on one line in most APA journals), the typesetter will break it. For long equations, indicate on the final version of the accepted manuscript where breaks would be acceptable.

4.17 Equations in Text

Place short and simple equations, such as $a = [(1 + b)/x]^{1/2}$, in the line of text. Equations in the line of text should not project above or below the line; for example, the equation above would be difficult to set in the line of text if it were in this form:

$$a = \sqrt{\frac{1+b}{x}}.$$

To present fractions in the line of text, use a slanted line (/) and appropriate parentheses, brackets, and braces: Use ( ) first, then [( )], and finally {[( )]}. Use parentheses and brackets to avoid ambiguity: Does $a/b + c$ mean $(a/b) + c$ or $a/(b + c)$?

4.18 Displayed Equations

Display simple equations if they must be numbered for later reference. Display all complex equations. Number all displayed equations consecutively, with the number in parentheses near the right margin of the page:

$$w_j \pm z_{1-\alpha/2}\hat{\sigma}_{w_j}. \tag{3}$$

When referring to numbered equations, write out the reference; for example, write *Equation 3* (do not abbreviate as *Eq. 3*), or write *the third equation*.

4.19 Preparing Statistical and Mathematical Copy

If possible, type all signs and symbols in mathematical copy. Supply as camera-ready copy any special symbols that cannot be produced by a word-processing program. Type fences (i.e., parentheses, brackets, and braces), uppercase and lowercase letters, punctuation, subscripts and superscripts, and all other elements exactly as you want them to appear in the published article. Follow the conventions for the use of symbols, equations, and reporting results presented in the earlier sections of this chapter.

Displaying Results

In this chapter, we discuss the purposes that data displays can serve and provide guidance on designing and preparing them so that they communicate most effectively. Tables and figures enable authors to present a large amount of information efficiently and to make their data more comprehensible. Tables usually show numerical values or textual information (e.g., lists of stimulus words) arranged in an orderly display of columns and rows. A figure may be a chart, a graph, a photograph, a drawing, or any other illustration or nontextual depiction. At times the boundary between tables and figures may be unclear; however, tables are almost always characterized by a row/column structure. Any type of illustration other than a table is referred to as a *figure*.

General Guidance on Tables and Figures
5.01 Purposes of Data Displays

Data displays can serve several purposes:

- **exploration:** the data contain a message, and you would like to learn what it is (exploratory data analysis and data mining techniques are examples of displays that are principally exploratory);

- **communication:** you have discovered the meaning contained in the data and want to tell others about it (this is the traditional purpose of most data displays in scientific documents);

- **calculation:** the display allows you to estimate some statistic or function of the data (nomographs are the archetype of this);

- **storage:** you can store data in a display for retrieval later, including the results of a study for later use in a meta-analysis (historically, this role has been fulfilled by tables, but figures sometimes serve this purpose more efficiently); and

- **decoration:** data displays attract attention, and you may choose to use them to make your manuscript more visually appealing (as in newspapers and other media reports).

In scientific publication, the communication function of graphical displays dominates; however, other features (e.g., storage) may be useful in a graphical representation.

5.02 Design and Preparation of a Data Display

The first step in preparing a display for submission is to determine the purposes of the display and the relative importance of those purposes. For example, the detail required for a storage display may conflict with the clarity required for a communicative one. Once you have decided on a display's hierarchy of purposes, choose the template best designed for its primary purpose—the *canonical form* of a display. Such a display (e.g., a scatterplot) has shown itself to be flexible (it works for many kinds of data), robust (it works reasonably well even when it is not exactly suitable), and adaptive (it shows a capacity for adaptation to make it suitable). Further, the use of canonical forms simplifies the task of readers trying to make sense of a display because they can rely on past experience with the form.

The preparation of graphic materials requires careful attention to organization and content. Graphical elements need to be edited with the same care as the textual elements of a manuscript. Changes in text often demand changes in graphical elements, and failure to edit graphical materials and to sharpen the focus of the display is a major shortcoming in much scientific writing.

Design your graphical display with the reader in mind; that is, remember the communicative function of the display.

- Place items that are to be compared next to each other.
- Place labels so that they clearly abut the elements they are labeling.
- Use fonts that are large enough to be read without the use of magnification.
- Include all of the information needed to understand it within the graphical image—avoid novel abbreviations, use table notes, and label graphical elements.
- Keep graphical displays free of extraneous materials, no matter how decorative those materials may make the graphic look.

Communication is the primary purpose of the graphic. An attractive graphical display makes a scientific article a more effective communication device.

5.03 Graphical Versus Textual Presentation

Be selective in choosing how many graphical elements to include in your paper. First, a reader may have difficulty sorting through a large number of tables and figures and may lose track of your message. Second, a disproportionately large number of tables and figures compared with a small amount of text can cause problems with the layout of typeset pages; text that is constantly broken up with tables will be hard for the reader to follow. Third, graphical presentations are not always optimal for effective communication. For example, the results of many standard statistical significance tests can often be effectively presented in text:

> The one-way ANOVA, $F(1, 136) = 4.86$, $MSE = 3.97$, $p = .029$, $\eta^2 = .03$, demonstrated statistically significant differences between the two groups, as theory would dictate.

Information that used to be routinely presented in tables (e.g., analysis of variance [ANOVA] tables) is now routinely presented in text.

5.04 Formatting Tables and Figures

Most manuscripts are now submitted electronically; therefore, all the elements of the manuscript must be in electronic format. These elements may be produced in many different file formats (e.g., .doc, .jpg, .pps, .pdf), and any publisher may limit the formats it accepts. Most tables are constructed with the tables feature of the word-processing program used to generate the manuscript text. However, tables are sometimes cut and pasted from computer outputs (rarely recommended) or may be PDF images created from scans of tables prepared in other ways. When tables are prepared with standard word-processing programs, the text can be converted directly into typographic files, thereby lowering the probability of typesetting errors.

Figures are generally submitted in a variety of formats, as is necessitated by the multiple ways in which they are produced. Often, figures such as graphs and charts are initially produced with presentation software such as Microsoft PowerPoint. Photographic elements are generally limited to specific image formats that allow for clear resolution of the image in its printed application. As a rule, figures are reproduced in the print version of articles as they are received from the author (following any editorial changes approved by the editor).

For publishers that offer online supplemental archives, carefully delineate the materials that will appear with the article from those that will be placed in the online supplemental archive (see section 6.04). Because of the relatively high cost of color reproduction, include it only when the color representation adds significantly to the understanding of the material. If color representation is not crucial for immediate understanding, you may consider placing it online as supplemental material.

5.05 Table and Figure Numbers

Number all tables and figures with Arabic numerals in the order in which they are first mentioned in text, regardless of whether a more detailed discussion of the table or figure occurs later in the paper. Do not use suffix letters to number tables and figures; that is, label them as Table 5, Table 6, and Table 7 or Figure 5, Figure 6, and Figure 7 instead of 5, 5a, and 5b. If the manuscript includes an appendix with tables or figures, identify those elements of the appendix with capital letters and Arabic numerals (e.g., Table A1 is the first table of Appendix A or of a sole appendix that is not labeled with a letter; Figure C2 is the second figure of Appendix C).

5.06 Permission to Reproduce Data Displays

If you reproduced or adapted a table, figure, questionnaire, or test item from a copyrighted source, you must obtain written permission for print and electronic reuse from the copyright holder and give credit in the table or figure caption to the original author and copyright holder. A number of commercial instruments—for example, intelligence tests and projective measures—are highly protected. Permission is required, and may be denied, to republish even one item from such instruments. Any reproduced table (or figure) or part thereof must be accompanied by a note at the bottom of the reprinted table (or in the figure caption) giving credit to the original author and to the copyright holder (see section 6.01 for the correct wording of copyright permission footnotes). For detailed information on copyright and permissions, see section 7.10.

Tables

When planning tables for inclusion in a manuscript, determine (a) the data readers will need to understand the discussion and (b) the data necessary to provide the "sufficient set of statistics" (see section 4.14) to support the use of the inferential methods used.

5.07 Conciseness in Tables

Limit the content of your tables to essential materials. Tables with surplus elements are less effective than lean tables. The principle of conciseness is relevant not only for text tables but also for tables to be placed in online supplemental archives. Although supplemental tables may be longer and more detailed than text tables, they must be directly and clearly related to the content of the article (see section 6.04). Tables should be integral to the text but should be designed so that they can be understood in isolation.

5.08 Table Layout

The basic components of a prototypical table are shown in Table 5.1, including the technical term, location, and definition of each element.

Table layout should be logical and easily grasped by the reader. Table entries that are to be compared should be next to one another. Following this principle, in general, different indices (e.g., means, standard deviations, sample sizes) should be segregated into different parts or lines of tables. Position variable and condition labels in close proximity to the values of the variable to facilitate comparison. Table 5.2 illustrates these principles.

All tables are meant to show something specific; for example, tables that communicate quantitative data are effective only when the data are arranged so that their meaning is obvious at a glance (Wainer, 1997). Often, the same data can be arranged in different ways to emphasize different features of the data. In Table 5.3, the same factor loading data are displayed in two different

■ Table 5.1. Basic Components of a Table

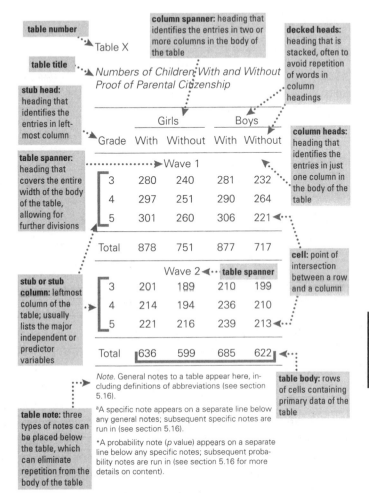

table number → Table X

column spanner: heading that identifies the entries in two or more columns in the body of the table

decked heads: heading that is stacked, often to avoid repetition of words in column headings

table title → Numbers of Children With and Without Proof of Parental Citizenship

stub head: heading that identifies the entries in leftmost column

column heads: heading that identifies the entries in just one column in the body of the table

table spanner: heading that covers the entire width of the body of the table, allowing for further divisions

stub or stub column: leftmost column of the table; usually lists the major independent or predictor variables

cell: point of intersection between a row and a column

table note: three types of notes can be placed below the table, which can eliminate repetition from the body of the table

table body: rows of cells containing primary data of the table

Grade	Girls		Boys	
	With	Without	With	Without
Wave 1				
3	280	240	281	232
4	297	251	290	264
5	301	260	306	221
Total	878	751	877	717
Wave 2				
3	201	189	210	199
4	214	194	236	210
5	221	216	239	213
Total	636	599	685	622

Note. General notes to a table appear here, including definitions of abbreviations (see section 5.16).

[a]A specific note appears on a separate line below any general notes; subsequent specific notes are run in (see section 5.16).

*A probability note (*p* value) appears on a separate line below any specific notes; subsequent probability notes are run in (see section 5.16 for more details on content).

ways. The first example emphasizes the factor structure of the two test batteries by keeping the subscales of the batteries adjacent to each other. The second arrangement of the same data emphasizes the nature of the factors by grouping the subscales of the test batteries according to the pattern of the factor loadings. Which arrangement is better depends on your purpose.

■ **Table 5.2.** Sample of Effective Table Layout

Table X

Proportion of Errors in Younger and Older Groups

Level of difficulty		Younger			Older	
	n	*M* (*SD*)	95% CI	*n*	*M* (*SD*)	95% CI
Low	12	.05 (.08)	[.02, .11]	18	.14 (.15)	[.08, .22]
Moderate	15	.05 (.07)	[.02, .10]	12	.17 (.15)	[.08, .28]
High	16	.11 (.10)	[.07, .17]	14	.26 (.21)	[.15, .39]

Note. CI = confidence interval.

5.09 Standard Forms

Some data tables have certain standard (canonical) forms. The advantage of using the canonical form is that the reader generally knows where to look in the table for certain kinds of information. In some situations, one may want to use a format other than the canonical table form to make a specific point or to stress certain relationships. The judicious use of nonstandard forms can be effective but must always be motivated by the special circumstances of the data array. When using nonstandard forms, make certain that labeling is extremely clear because most readers will assume that the canonical form is being used. Section 5.18 includes examples of standard tables for presenting several types of data.

5.10 Relation of Tables and Text

Discussing tables in text. An informative table supplements—rather than duplicates—the text. In the text, refer to every table and tell the reader what to look for. Discuss only the table's highlights; if you find yourself discussing every item of the table in the text, the table is unnecessary. If tables are to be submitted for online supplemental archives, mention their existence only briefly

■ Table 5.3. Sample Factor Loadings Table (With Rotation Method Specified)

The following table is formatted to emphasize the structure of the test batteries.

Table X

Factor Loadings for Exploratory Factor Analysis With Varimax Rotation of Personality Pathology Scales

Scale	Introversion	Emotional Dysregulation	Peculiarity
SPQ Constricted Affect	**.77**	.33	.21
Excessive Social Anxiety	**.43**	**.52**	.29
Ideas of Reference	−.08	.17	**.67**
No Friends	**.84**	.19	.13
Odd Beliefs	−.03	.13	**.50**
Odd Behavior	.23	.19	**.56**
Odd Speech	.15	.34	**.56**
Unusual Perceptions	.09	.14	**.76**
DAPP Submissiveness	.24	**.70**	.11
Cognitive Distortion	.26	**.70**	.36
Identity Problems	**.52**	**.58**	.16
Affective Lability	.11	**.73**	.34
Restricted Expression	**.69**	.31	.02
Passive Oppositionality	.25	**.70**	.12
Intimacy Problems	**.63**	.18	.03
Anxiousness	.24	**.83**	.18
Conduct Problems	.27	.10	.24
Suspiciousness	.39	.36	.23
Social Avoidance	**.59**	**.67**	.10
Insecure Attachment	.04	**.58**	.26
Self-Harm	.30	.38	.28

(continued)

■ Table 5.3. Sample Factor Loadings Table (continued)

Scale	Introversion	Emotional Dysregulation	Peculiarity
Chapman Magical			
Ideation	.12	.17	**.72**
Social Anhedonia	**.78**	.04	.26
Perceptual Aberrations	.12	.25	**.49**
Physical Anhedonia	**.61**	.05	−.15

Note. Factor loadings > .40 are in boldface. SPQ = Schizotypal Personality Questionnaire; DAPP = Dimensional Assessment of Personality Pathology—Basic Questionnaire.

The following table is formatted to emphasize the structure of the factors.

Table X

Factor Loadings for Exploratory Factor Analysis With Varimax Rotation of Personality Pathology Scales

Scale	Introversion	Emotional Dysregulation	Peculiarity
SPQ No Friends	**.84**	.19	.13
Chapman Social			
Anhedonia	**.78**	.04	.26
SPQ Constricted Affect	**.77**	.33	.21
DAPP Restricted			
Expression	**.69**	.31	.02
DAPP Intimacy Problems	**.63**	.18	.03
Chapman Physical			
Anhedonia	**.61**	.05	−.15
DAPP Social Avoidance	**.59**	**.67**	.10
DAPP Identity Problems	**.52**	**.58**	.16

(continued)

■ Table 5.3. Sample Factor Loadings Table (continued)

Scale	Introversion	Emotional Dysregulation	Peculiarity
SPQ Excessive Social Anxiety	**.43**	**.52**	.29
DAPP Anxiousness	.24	**.83**	.18
DAPP Affective Lability	.11	**.73**	.34
DAPP Cognitive Distortion	.26	**.70**	.36
DAPP Passive Oppositionality	.25	**.70**	.12
DAPP Submissiveness	.24	**.70**	.11
DAPP Insecure Attachment	.04	**.58**	.26
DAPP Self-Harm	.30	.38	.28
SPQ Unusual Perceptions	.09	.14	**.76**
Chapman Magical Ideation	.12	.17	**.72**
SPQ Ideas of Reference	−.08	.17	**.67**
SPQ Odd Speech	.15	.34	**.56**
SPQ Odd Behavior	.23	.19	**.56**
SPQ Odd Beliefs	−.03	.13	**.50**
Chapman Perceptual Aberrations	.12	.25	**.49**
DAPP Suspiciousness	.39	.36	.23
DAPP Conduct Problems	.27	.10	.24

Note. Factor loadings > .40 are in boldface. SPQ = Schizotypal Personality Questionnaire; DAPP = Dimensional Assessment of Personality Pathology—Basic Questionnaire. Adapted from "A Dimensional Model of Personality Disorder: Incorporating DSM Cluster A Characteristics," by J. L. Tackett, A. L. Silberschmidt, R. F. Krueger, and S. R. Sponheim, 2008, *Journal of Abnormal Psychology, 117,* p. 457. Copyright 2008 by the American Psychological Association.

in the print version of the article. Tables designated as supplemental materials must be accompanied by enough information to be completely understood on their own (see section 6.04).

Citing tables. In the text, refer to tables by their number:

> as shown in Table 8, the responses were provided by children with pretraining . . .

Do not write "the table above" (or below) or "the table on page 32," because the position and page number of a table cannot be determined until the pages are typeset.

5.11 Relation Between Tables

Consider combining tables that repeat data. Ordinarily, identical columns or rows of data should not appear in two or more tables. Be consistent in the presentations of all tables within a manuscript to facilitate comparisons. Use similar formats, titles, and headings, and use the same terminology throughout (e.g., *response time* or *reaction time*, not both).

5.12 Table Titles

Give every table a brief but clear and explanatory title. The basic content of the table should be easily inferred from the title.

Too general:

> Table 1
>
> *Relation Between College Majors and Performance* [It is unclear what data are presented in the table.]

Too detailed:

> Table 1
>
> *Mean Performance Scores on Test A, Test B, and Test C of Students With Psychology, Physics, English, and Engineering Majors* [This duplicates information in the headings of the table.]

Good title:

> Mean Performance Scores of Students With
> Different College Majors

Abbreviations that appear in the headings or the body of a table sometimes can be parenthetically explained in the table title.

> Hit and False-Alarm (FA) Proportions in
> Experiment 2

Explain abbreviations that require longer explanations or that do not relate to the table title in a general note to the table (see section 5.16 and Table 5.1). Do not use a specific footnote to clarify an element of the title.

5.13 Table Headings

A table classifies related items and enables the reader to compare them. Data form the body of the table. Headings establish your organization of the data and identify the columns of data beneath them. Like a table title, a heading should be brief and should not be many more characters in length than the widest entry.

Poor:	*Better:*
Grade level	Grade
3	3
4	4
5	5

You may use standard abbreviations and symbols for nontechnical terms (e.g., *no.* for *number*, % for *percent*) and for statistics (e.g., M, SD, χ^2, or any other abbreviation in Table 3.1) in table headings without explanation. Abbreviations of technical terms, group names, and the like must be explained in the table title or in a note to the table (see section 5.12). Abbreviations may also be explained parenthetically following entries in the stub column.

Each column of a table must have a heading, including the *stub column* or *stub*, which is the leftmost column of the table (see Table 5.1 for illustration of technical terms). Subordination within the stub is easier to comprehend if you indent the stub items rather than create an additional column (e.g., Tables 5.4 and 5.5). The stub usually lists the major independent or predictor variables. In Table 5.1, for instance, the stub lists the grades. Number

■ **Table 5.4.** Sample Table With Detailed Specifications of Complex Experimental Designs

Table X

Summary of Experimental Designs

Group	Stage I	Stage II	Test
Experiment 1			
Block	A+	AB+	B vs. D
		CD+	
Unblock intensity	A+	AB+	
		CD+	
Unblock number	A+	AB++	
		CD++	
Experiment 2	A+	AB+	AD vs. BC
	C+		
Experiment 3	A+		AD vs. BC
	B+		A, B, C, D
	C+		
	D++		
Experiment 4a	A+	AB+	AD vs. BC
	C+		
Experiment 4b	A+	AB++	AD vs. BC
	C+		
Experiment 5	A+	AB+	AD vs. BC
	C+	CD++	A, B, C, D

Note. A, B, C, and D were four conditioned stimuli: a clicker, tone, light, and flashing light, respectively (counterbalanced). + denotes a 0.4-mA shock unconditioned stimulus; ++ denotes two 0.4-mA shocks; **+** denotes a 0.8-mA unconditioned stimulus. Adapted from "Unblocking in Pavlovian Fear Conditioning," by L. Bradfield and G. P. McNally, 2008, *Journal of Experimental Psychology: Animal Behavior Processes, 34,* p. 259. Copyright 2008 by the American Psychological Association.

■■■ **Table 5.5.** Sample Table Display of a Sample's
Characteristics

Table X

*Individual and Family Characteristics as a Percentage of the Sample
(Census Data in Parentheses)*

Characteristic	Mother (n = 750)	Father (n = 466)	Child (n = 750)
Self-identity			
Mexican	77.2	71.0	41.0
Mexican American	22.8	29.0	59.0
Nativity[a]			
Mexico	74.2 (38.2)	80.0 (44.2)	29.7
United States	25.8 (61.8)	20.0 (55.8)	70.3
Language preference[b]			
English	30.2 (52.7)	23.2 (52.7)	82.5 (70.0)
Spanish	69.8 (48.3)	76.8 (48.3)	17.5 (30.0)
Education level completed[a]			
8th grade or less	29.2 (30.7)	30.2 (33.4)	
Some high school	19.5 (20.9)	22.4 (22.6)	
12th grade	23.1 (22.5)	20.9 (20.7)	
Some college/ vocational training	22.0 (19.2)	20.2 (17.1)	
Bachelor's or higher	6.2 (6.8)	6.2 (6.2)	
Employment status[c]			
Employed	63.6 (46.6)	96.6 (97.1)	
Unemployed	11.2 (3.5)	3.5 (2.9)	
Housewife	25.2		

Note. Adapted from "Sampling and Recruitment in Studies of Cultural Influences on
Adjustment: A Case Study With Mexican Americans," by M. W. Roosa, F. F. Liu, M. Torres,
N. A. Gonzales, G. P. Knight, and D. Saenz, 2008, *Journal of Family Psychology, 22,* p. 300.
Copyright 2008 by the American Psychological Association.
[a]Census data are for all women or men and are not limited to parents or adults in our age
group. [b]The most comparable census data for mothers and fathers are for all adults 18 and
older and for children are for 15- to 17-year-olds. [c]Census data are for all women, not just
mothers, whereas the male data are limited to husbands.

elements only when they appear in a correlation matrix (see Table 5.6) or if they are referred to by number in text.

All headings identify items below them, not across from them. The headings just above the body of the table (called *column heads* and *column spanners*) identify the entries in the vertical columns in the body of the table. A column head covers just one column; a column spanner covers two or more columns, each with its own column head. Headings stacked in this way are called *decked heads*. Often decked heads can be used to avoid repetition of words in column heads (see Table 5.1). If possible, do not use more than two levels of decked heads.

■ **Table 5.6.** Sample Table of Correlations in Which the Values for Two Samples Are Presented

Table X

Summary of Intercorrelations, Means, and Standard Deviations for Scores on the BSS, BDI, SAFE, and MEIM as a Function of Race

Measure	1	2	3	4	M	SD
1. BSS	—	.54*	.29*	−.23*	1.31	4.32
2. BDI	.54*	—	.34*	−.14*	8.33	7.76
3. SAFE	.19*	.30*	—	−.074	47.18	13.24
4. MEIM	−.09	−.11	−.08	—	47.19	6.26
M	1.50	9.13	39.07	37.78		
SD	3.84	7.25	13.17	7.29		

Note. Intercorrelations for African American participants ($n = 296$) are presented above the diagonal, and intercorrelations for European American participants ($n = 163$) are presented below the diagonal. Means and standard deviations for African American students are presented in the vertical columns, and means and standard deviations for European Americans are presented in the horizontal rows. For all scales, higher scores are indicative of more extreme responding in the direction of the construct assessed. BSS = Beck Suicide Scale; BDI = Beck Depression Inventory; SAFE = Societal, Attitudinal, Familial, and Environmental Acculturative Stress Scale; MEIM = Multigroup Ethnic Identity Measure. Adapted from "An Empirical Investigation of Acculturative Stress and Ethnic Identity as Moderators for Depression and Suicidal Ideation in College Students," by R. L. Walker, L. R. Wingate, E. M. Obasi, and T. E. Joiner, 2008, *Cultural Diversity and Ethnic Minority Psychology, 14,* p. 78. Copyright 2008 by the American Psychological Association. $*p < .01$.

Incorrect:

Temporal lobe:	Left	Right

Wordy:

Left temporal lobe	Right temporal lobe

Correct:

Temporal lobe	
Left	Right

A few tables may require *table spanners* in the body of the table. These table spanners cover the entire width of the body of the table, allowing for further divisions within the table (see Tables 5.1 and 5.15). Also, table spanners can be used to combine two tables provided they have identical column heads.

Any item within a column should be syntactically as well as conceptually comparable with the other items in that column, and all items should be described by the column head:

Nonparallel:

Condition
Functional psychotic
Drinks to excess
Character disorder

Parallel:

Condition
Functional psychosis
Alcoholism
Character disorder

Stub heads, column heads, and column spanners should be singular unless they refer to groups (e.g., *Children*), but table spanners may be plural. Capitalize only the first letter of the first word of all headings (column heads, column spanners, stub heads, and table spanners) and word entries. Also, capitalize the first letter of each word of all proper nouns and the first word following a colon or em dash.

■■■ **Table 5.7.** Sample Table of Results of Fitting Mathematical Models

Table X

Estimates [and 95% Confidence Intervals] for the Parameters of the Simplified Conjoint Recognition Model for Experiment 5

| Parameter | List condition | | | $G^2_{(df=2)}$ | p |
	Target-first	Target-last	Control		
a	.43 [.30, .57]	.28 [.16, .40]	.24 [.10, .38]	4.26	.12
b	.26 [.19, .32]	.27 [.21, .33]	.19 [.13, .24]	4.68	.10
G_t	.29 [.00, .63]	.38 [.14, .63]	.28 [.03, .53]	0.39	.82
G_r	.43 [.19, .67]	.70 [.55, .84]	.72 [.56, .88]	4.86	.09
V_t	.89 [.83, .94]	.81 [.75, .87]	.86 [.80, .91]	3.20	.20
V_r	.72$_a$ [61, .82]	.05$_b$ [.00, .42]	.23$_b$ [.00, .62]	20.89	<.01

Note. Parameter estimates in each row that share subscripts do not differ significantly. a = probability of guessing "target"; b = probability of guessing that an item is either a target or a related probe; G_t = probability of retrieving a target's gist trace given a target probe; G_r = probability of retrieving a target's gist trace given a related probe; V_t = probability of retrieving a target's verbatim trace given a target probe; V_r = probability of retrieving a target's verbatim trace given a related probe. Adapted from "A Simplified Conjoint Recognition Paradigm for the Measurement of Gist and Verbatim Memory," by C. Stahl and K. C. Klauer, 2008, *Journal of Experimental Psychology: Learning, Memory, and Cognition, 34,* p. 579. Copyright 2008 by the American Psychological Association.

5.14 Table Body

Decimal values. The table body contains the data. Express numerical values to the number of decimal places that the precision of measurement justifies (see section 4.05), and if possible, carry all comparable values to the same number of decimal places.

Empty cells. If the point of intersection between a row and a column (called a *cell*) cannot be filled because data are not applicable, leave the cell blank. If a cell cannot be filled because data were not obtained or are not reported, insert a dash in that cell and explain the use of the dash in the general note to the table. By convention, a dash in the main diagonal position of a correlation matrix (see Table 5.6) indicates the correlation of an item with itself, which must be 1.00, and is simply replaced by the dash. If you need to explain that an element of a table is unavailable or inapplicable, use a specific note rather than a dash (see section 5.16).

Conciseness. Be selective in your presentation. Do not include columns of data that can be calculated easily from other columns:

Not concise:

	No. responses			
Participant	First trial	Second trial	Total	*M*
1	5	7	12	6

The example could be improved by giving either the number of responses per trial or the total number of responses, whichever is more important to the discussion, and by not including the column with the mean because its calculation is simple.

5.15 Confidence Intervals in Tables

When a table includes point estimates, for example, means, correlations, or regression slopes, it should also, where possible, include confidence intervals. You may report confidence intervals in tables either by using brackets, as in text (see section 2.11) and in Table 5.8, or by giving lower and upper limits in separate columns, as in Table 5.9. In every table that includes confidence intervals, state the confidence level, for example, 95%. It is usually best to use the same confidence level throughout a paper.

■ **Table 5.8.** Sample Table Indicating
Confidence Intervals With Brackets

Table X

*Weight Status, Body Dissatisfaction, and Weight Control Behaviors
at Time 1 and Suicidal Ideation at Time 2*

Variable	Unadjusted[a]		Adjusted for demographic variables[b]	
	OR	95% CI	*OR*	95% CI
Weight status				
Young men	0.97	[0.78, 1.21]	0.94	[0.75, 1.19]
Young women	1.06	[0.88, 1.26]	1.02	[0.85, 1.23]
Body dissatisfaction				
Young men	0.88	[0.50, 1.54]	0.99	[0.56, 1.75]
Young women	1.06	[0.77, 1.46]	1.02	[0.74, 1.42]
UWCB				
Young men	0.81	[0.54, 1.24]	0.77	[0.50, 1.19]
Young women	0.89	[0.65, 1.21]	0.93	[0.68, 1.27]
EWCB				
Young men	1.36	[0.55, 3.36]	1.73	[0.69, 4.37]
Young women	1.98	[1.34, 2.93]	2.00	[1.34, 2.99]

Note. OR = odds ratio; CI = confidence interval; UWCB = unhealthy weight control behaviors; EWCB = extreme weight control behaviors. Adapted from "Are Body Dissatisfaction, Eating Disturbance, and Body Mass Index Predictors of Suicidal Behavior in Adolescents? A Longitudinal Study," by S. Crow, M. E. Eisenberg, M. Story, and D. Neumark-Sztainer, 2008, *Journal of Consulting and Clinical Psychology, 76,* p. 890. Copyright 2008 by the American Psychological Association.
[a]Four weight-related variables entered simultaneously. [b]Adjusted for race, socioeconomic status, and age group.

5.16 Table Notes

Tables may have three kinds of notes placed below the body of the table: general notes, specific notes, and probability notes.

A *general note* qualifies, explains, or provides information relating to the table as a whole and ends with an

■ **Table 5.9.** Sample Table Indicating Confidence Intervals With Upper and Lower Limits

Table X

Estimated Distance (cm) for Letter and Digit Stimuli

| Condition | $M(SD)$ | 95% CI | |
		LL	UL
Letters	14.5 (28.6)	5.4	23.6
Digits	31.8 (33.2)	21.2	42.4

Note. CI = confidence interval; *LL* = lower limit; *UL* = upper limit.

explanation of any abbreviations, symbols, and the like. Included within general notes would be any acknowledgments that a table is reproduced from another source. General notes are designated by the word *Note* (italicized) followed by a period. (See Tables 5.1 and 5.4, among others.)

> *Note.* Factor loadings greater than .45 are shown in boldface. M = match process; N = nonmatch process.

A *specific note* refers to a particular column, row, or cell. Specific notes are indicated by superscript lowercase letters (e.g., [a, b, c]). Within the headings and table body, order the superscripts from left to right and from top to bottom, starting at the top left.

Table notes, general or specific, apply only to that specific table and not to any other table. Begin each table's first footnote with a superscript lowercase *a* (see Table 5.5).

> [a]n = 25. [b]This participant did not complete the trials.

A *probability note* indicates how asterisks and other symbols are used in a table to indicate p values and thus the results of tests of statistical hypothesis testing. For results of statistical significance testing in text and tables, report the exact probabilities to two or three decimal places (e.g., $p = .023$ as opposed to $p < .05$; see Table 5.7 and section 4.05). When displaying the result in graphical modes (including certain tables such as tables of correlation matrices), it may be difficult to follow this recommendation without making the graphic unruly. Therefore, when displaying results graphically, revert to reporting in the "$p <$" style if using exact probabilities would make it difficult to comprehend the graphic. When discussing the results in the text, use exact probabilities regardless of the display mode. Include a probability note only when relevant to specific data within the table.

If the "$p <$" style is required, asterisks indicate ranges of p values. Assign the same number of asterisks from table to table within your paper, such as $^*p < .05$, $^{**}p < .01$, and $^{***}p < .001$. Do not use any value smaller than $^{***}p < .001$.

If you need to distinguish between one-tailed and two-tailed tests in the same table, use an asterisk for the two-tailed p values and an alternate symbol (e.g., dagger) for the one-tailed p values.

> $^*p < .05$, two-tailed. $^{**}p < .01$, two-tailed. $^\dagger p < .05$, one-tailed.
>
> $^{\dagger\dagger}p < .01$, one-tailed.

To indicate statistically significant differences between two or more table entries—for example, means that are compared with procedures such as a Tukey test—use lowercase subscripts (see Table 5.7). Explain the use of the subscripts in the table note (see the following sample table notes).

> *Note.* Means sharing a common subscript are not statistically different at $\alpha = .01$ according to the Tukey HSD procedure.

Order the notes to a table in the following sequence: general note, specific note, probability note (see Table 5.1).

> *Note.* The participants . . . responses.
>
> [a]$n = 25$. [b]$n = 42$.
>
> [*]$p < .05$. [**]$p < .01$.

Each type of note begins flush left (i.e., no paragraph indentation) on a new line below the table. The first specific note begins flush left on a new line under the general note; subsequent specific notes are run in (lengthy specific notes may be set on separate lines when typeset). The first probability note begins flush left on a new line; subsequent probability notes are run in.

Notes can be useful for eliminating repetition from the body of a table. Certain types of information may be appropriate either in the table or in a note. To determine the placement of such material, remember that clearly and efficiently organized data enable the reader to focus on the data. Thus, if probability values or subsample sizes are numerous, use a column rather than many notes. Conversely, if a row or column contains few entries (or the same entry), eliminate the column by adding a note to the table:

Poor:

Group	n
Anxious	15
Depressed	15
Control	15

Better:

Group[a]
Anxious
Depressed
Control

[a]$n = 15$

5.17 Ruling of Tables

Limit the use of *rules* (i.e., lines) in a table to those that are necessary for clarity. Appropriately positioned white space can be an effective substitute for rules; for example, long, uninterrupted columns of numbers or words are more readable if a horizontal line of space is inserted after every fourth or fifth entry. In the manuscript, use spacing between columns and rows and strict alignment to clarify relationships within a table.

Tables may be submitted either single- or double-spaced. Consider the readability of the table during the review process in making your decision.

5.18 Presenting Data in Specific Types of Tables

Complex experimental designs can be summarized in compact tables, making the entire structure of the experiment clear without the need for lengthy textual descriptions (see Table 5.4).

Important characteristics of a sample can be concisely summarized in a well-organized table. Providing comparable census data can help the reader understand the generalizability of the results (see Table 5.5).

Key psychometric properties of the major variables can be easily summarized in a table (see Table 5.10). Clearly state the index of reliability (or other psychometric property) being used and the sample on which the reliability was based (if different from the study sample).

Table 5.11 shows one-degree-of-freedom within-subject contrasts within a larger set of effects, including both confidence intervals and effect sizes. In Table 5.6, note the compact, yet information-packed, form in which the intercorrelations among the variables for two different groups are presented in the same table—one group below the main diagonal, the other above the main diagonal. Means and standard deviations for the two groups are similarly positioned, with the Group 1 means and standard deviations given in the last two data columns and those for Group 2 in the last two data rows. Construction of a correlation matrix of this type not only is concise in terms of the amount of page space used but also makes the visual comparison of correlational elements much easier.

Clearly label the type of regression (e.g., hierarchical) and type of regression coefficients (raw or standardized)

■ **Table 5.10.** Sample Table Display of Psychometric Properties of Key Outcome Variables

Table X

Psychometric Properties of the Major Study Variables

Variable	n	M	SD	α	Range Potential	Range Actual	Skew
Dispositional affectivity							
Positive	560	3.27	0.77	.91	1–5	1.0–5.0	−0.36
Negative	563	2.26	0.79	.91	1–5	1.0–4.7	0.63
Social support							
Mother	160	4.17	1.08	.92	1–5	1.0–5.0	−1.54
Partner	474	4.03	1.19	.94	1–5	1.0–5.0	−1.26
Friend	396	4.37	0.89	.90	1–5	1.0–5.0	−1.94
Social conflict							
Mother	159	1.22	0.47	.81	1–5	1.0–3.6	3.07
Partner	471	1.40	0.79	.90	1–5	1.0–5.0	2.63
Friend	381	1.15	0.45	.79	1–5	1.0–5.0	5.27
Postabortion adjustment							
Distress	609	0.59	0.63	.90	0–4	0.0–3.0	1.56
Well-being	606	4.60	0.69	.85	1–6	2.3–6.0	−0.53

Note. The variation in *sample size* is due to the variation in the number of women who told a particular source about the abortion. Adapted from "Mixed Messages: Implications of Social Conflict and Social Support Within Close Relationships for Adjustment to a Stressful Life Event," by B. Major, J. M. Zubek, M. L. Cooper, C. Cozzarelli, and C. Richards, 1997, *Journal of Personality and Social Psychology, 76,* p. 1355. Copyright 1997 by the American Psychological Association.

being reported (see Tables 5.12 and 5.13). For hierarchical and other sequential regressions, be sure to provide the increments of change (see section 4.14).

In model-comparison tables, ensure that the competing models are clearly identified and that the comparisons are clearly specified. Comparative fit indices can be useful for the reader (see Tables 5.14 and 5.15).

Table 5.11. Sample Table of One-Degree-of-Freedom Statistical Contrasts

Table X

Contrast of Time 1 With Time 2 For Exhaustion-Only Group That Changed Toward Burnout

Variable	Time 1		Time 2		t(34)	p	95% CI		Cohen's d
	M	SD	M	SD			LL	UL	
Workload	2.79	0.89	2.61	0.66	1.61	.12	−0.06	0.42	0.72
Control	3.60	0.83	3.13	1.18	1.91	.06	−0.05	0.98	0.85
Reward	3.58	0.82	3.26	0.62	1.68	.10	−0.08	0.70	0.75
Community	3.75	0.79	3.21	1.01	2.96	.006	0.16	0.92	1.32
Fairness	2.77	0.65	2.32	0.97	2.33	.03	0.05	0.85	1.04
Values	3.25	0.78	2.65	0.93	3.70	<.001	0.26	0.94	1.65
Exhaustion	3.16	0.96	3.62	0.95	−2.08	.05	−0.92	0.00	−0.93
Cynicism	0.92	0.38	3.30	1.05	−8.71	<.001	−2.95	−1.81	−3.89
Efficacy	4.54	1.08	4.38	1.25	0.51	.61	−0.49	0.80	0.23

Note. CI = confidence interval; LL = lower limit; UL = upper limit. Adapted from "Early Predictors of Job Burnout and Engagement," by C. Maslach and M. Leiter, 2008, *Journal of Applied Psychology, 93*, p. 509. Copyright 2008 by the American Psychological Association.

■ **Table 5.12.** Sample Regression Table

Table X

Predictors of Self-Reported Moral Behavior

	Self-reported moral behavior		
		Model 2	
	Model 1		
Variable	B	B	95% CI
Constant	3.192**	2.99**	[2.37, 3.62]
Gender	0.18*	0.17	[−0.00, 0.33]
Age	−0.06	−0.05	[−0.14, 0.03]
Social desirability bias	−0.08**	−0.08**	[−0.10, −0.05]
Moral identity internalization	−0.17**	−0.16**	[−0.26, −0.06]
Moral identity symbolization	0.07*	0.06	[−0.01, 0.12]
Perceptual moral attentiveness		0.07*	[0.00, 0.13]
Reflective moral attentiveness		−0.01	[−0.08, 0.06]
R^2	.29	.31	
F	19.07**	14.46**	
ΔR^2		.01	
ΔF		2.39	

Note. N = 242. CI = confidence interval. Adapted from "Moral Attentiveness: Who Pays Attention to the Moral Aspects of Life?" by S. J. Reynolds, 2008, *Journal of Applied Psychology, 93*, p. 1035. Copyright 2008 by the American Psychological Association.
*p < .05. **p < .01.

The two illustrative samples in Table 5.3 demonstrate how table formatting can be varied depending on the emphasis desired. Tables may contain entries other than just numerals (e.g., text; see Table 5.16) as long as the basic row by column structure is maintained.

■ Table 5.13. Sample Hierarchical Multiple Regression Table

Table X

Hierarchical Multiple Regression Analyses Predicting Postabortion Positive Well-Being From Preabortion Social Support and Preabortion Social Conflict With Mother, Partner, and Friend

| | Source of social support and social conflict | | | | | |
| | Mother | | Partner | | Friend | |
Predictor	ΔR^2	β	ΔR^2	β	ΔR^2	β
Step 1 Control variables[a]	.13*		.10***		.10***	
Step 2 Positive affect	.16***	.31***	.19***	.32***	.22***	.35***
Negative affect		−.25***		−.27***		−.30***
Step 3 Social support	.02	.17*	.05***	.17***	.01*	.08†
Social conflict		.09		−.08		−.06
Step 4 Social Support × Social Conflict	.01	−.14	.00	−.00	.00	−.07
Total R^2	.32***		.33***		.34***	
n	153		455		373	

Note. Adapted from "Mixed Messages: Implications of Social Conflict and Social Support Within Close Relationships for Adjustment to a Stressful Life Event," by B. Major, J. M. Zubek, M. L. Cooper, C. Cozzarelli, and C. Richards, 1997, *Journal of Personality and Social Psychology, 72,* p. 1359. Copyright 1997 by the American Psychological Association.
[a]Control variables included age, race, education, marital status, religion, abortion history, depression history, and prior mental health counseling.
†$p < .10$. *$p < .05$. ***$p < .001$.

■ Table 5.14. Sample Model Comparison Table

Table X

Fit Indices for Nested Sequence of Cross-Sectional Models

Model	χ^2	NFI	PFI	χ^2_{diff}	ΔNFI
1. Mobley's (1977) measurement model	443.18*	.92	.67		
2. Quit & search intentions	529.80*	.89	.69		
Difference between Model 2 and Model 1				86.61*	.03
3. Search intentions & thoughts of quitting	519.75*	.90	.69		
Difference between Model 3 and Model 1				76.57*	.02
4. Intentions to quit & thoughts of quitting	546.97*	.89	.69		
Difference between Model 4 and Model 1				103.78*	.03
5. One withdrawal cognition	616.97*	.87	.70		
Difference between Model 5 and Model 1				173.79*	.05
6. Hom, Griffeth, & Sallaro's (1984) structural model	754.37*	.84	.71		
Difference between Model 6 and Model 5				137.39*	.03

(continued)

▇ Table 5.14. Sample Model Comparison Table (continued)

Model	χ^2	NFI	PFI	χ^2_{diff}	ΔNFI
7. Structural null model	2,741.49*	.23	.27		
Difference between Model 7 and Model 6				1,987.13*	.61
8. Null model	3,849.07*				

Note. NFI = normed fit index; PFI = parsimonious fit index. Adapted from "Structural Equations Modeling Test of a Turnover Theory: Cross-Sectional and Longitudinal Analyses," by P. W. Hom and R. W. Griffeth, 1991, *Journal of Applied Psychology, 76,* p. 356. Copyright 1991 by the American Psychological Association.
*$p < .05$.

Table 5.15. Sample Multilevel Model Table

Table X

Fixed Effects Estimates (Top) and Variance–Covariance Estimates (Bottom) for Models of the Predictors of Positive Parenting

Parameter	Model 1	Model 2	Model 3	Model 4	Model 5
			Fixed effects		
Intercept	12.51 (0.04)	12.23 (0.07)	12.23 (0.07)	12.23 (0.07)	12.64 (0.11)
Level 1 (child-specific)					
Age		−0.49* (0.02)	−0.48* (0.02)	−0.48* (0.02)	−0.48* (0.02)
Age^2		0.06* (0.01)	0.06* (0.01)	0.06* (0.01)	0.06* (0.01)
Negative affectivity		−0.56* (0.08)	−0.53* (0.08)	−0.57* (0.09)	−0.57* (0.09)
Girl		0.05 (0.05)	0.05 (0.05)	0.04 (0.05)	0.07 (0.05)
Not bio. mother		−0.34 (0.26)	−0.28 (0.26)	−0.28 (0.26)	−0.30 (0.28)
Not bio. father		−0.34* (0.10)	−0.31* (0.10)	−0.30* (0.10)	−0.29 (0.15)
Oldest sibling		0.38* (0.07)	0.37* (0.07)	0.37* (0.07)	0.36* (0.07)

(continued)

Table 5.15. Sample Multilevel Model Table (continued)

Parameter	Model 1	Model 2	Model 3	Model 4	Model 5
Middle sibling		0.36* (0.06)	0.34* (0.06)	0.35* (0.06)	0.28* (0.06)
Level 2 (family)					
SES					0.18* (0.06)
Marital dissatisfaction					−0.43* (0.14)
Family size					−0.41* (0.08)
Single parent					0.09 (0.19)
All-girl sibship					−0.20 (0.13)
Mixed-gender sibship					−0.25* (0.10)

	Random parameters				
Level 2					
Intercept/intercept (s_{a0}^2)	5.13* (0.17)	4.87* (0.15)	4.92* (0.15)	4.86* (0.15)	4.79* (0.14)
Age/age (s_{a1}^2)			0.09* (0.01)	0.09* (0.01)	0.09* (0.01)
Age/intercept (s_{a10}^2)			−0.04 (0.03)	−0.05 (0.03)	−0.05 (0.03)
Neg. affect/neg. affect (s_{a3}^2)				1.51* (0.46)	1.51* (0.46)
Neg. affect/intercept (s_{a30l}^2)				−0.03 (0.20)	−0.02 (0.20)
Neg. affect/age (s_{a31l}^2)				0.00 (0.05)	0.00 (0.05)
Level 1					
Intercept/intercept (w_0)	3.80* (0.08)	2.74* (0.06)	2.30* (0.07)	2.19* (0.07)	2.18* (0.07)
−2*log likelihood	38,369.7	37,001.9	36,919.6	36,899.8	36,849.4

Note. Standard errors are in parentheses. Not bio. mother = not living with the biological mother; Not bio. father = not living with the biological father; SES = socioeconomic status; Neg. affect = negative affectivity. Adapted from "The Role of the Shared Family Context in Differential Parenting," by J. M. Jenkins, J. Rasbash, and T. G. O'Connor, 2003, *Developmental Psychology, 39*, p. 104. Copyright 2003 by the American Psychological Association.
*$p < .05$.

Table 5.16. Sample Word Table

Table X

Inductively Developed Thematic Categories

Category	Thematic category	Key terms	Characteristic Level 3 responses
Q1. How "should" husbands, wives, and children act? What is the "right way" to act? What are certain family members supposed to do?			
Family traditionalism			
F1	Macho privilege	Man, woman, say, house OR mother	The husband is the one who gives "orders." The wife never says what she feels. The children should "obey," no matter what.
F2	Family trust and respect	Respect OR trust OR work OR help	Always share everything equally and there should be respect among everyone/between couples and children.
F3	Family unity	Family OR unity	Above all, there should be family unity.
F4	Values traditions	Tradition OR continue OR important	If she is a true believer, she should always participate in the traditions.

Q2. Many "traditional" people like Maria believe that life in a small rural town **is** better than life in a big city. Please tell me some of these beliefs.

Rural lifestyle

R1	Small town life is better	Small town OR everybody knows each other	Because there is so much violence in the big city. . . . You know your town and people and you trust each other like family.
R2	Big city opportunities	Live OR believe OR big cities OR better	Better to live in a big city because there are more jobs and educational opportunities.
R3	Rural tranquility	Life OR less stress OR rural	I agree that life in a small town is better because in a small town life is more peaceful. There is less gang activity and overall life is more peaceful.
R4	It depends	It depends OR more opportunities OR the city	Sometimes it is true that rural life is better. However, it's also true that a big city can help you or can destroy you; that depends on you.

Note. Adapted from "Traditions and Alcohol Use: A Mixed-Methods Analysis," by F. G. Castro and K. Coe, 2007, *Cultural Diversity and Ethnic Minority Psychology, 13,* p. 276. Copyright 2007 by the American Psychological Association.

5.19 Table Checklist

The following checklist may help ensure that the data in your table are effectively presented and conform to the style rules presented in this chapter.

■ Table Checklist

☐ Is the table necessary?

☐ Does it belong in the print version of the article, or can it go in an online supplemental file?

☐ Are all comparable tables in the manuscript consistent in presentation?

☐ Is the title brief but explanatory?

☐ Does every column have a column head?

☐ Are all abbreviations explained, as well as special use of italics, parentheses, dashes, boldface, and special symbols?

☐ Are the notes in the following order: general note, specific note, probability note?

☐ Are all vertical rules eliminated?

☐ Are confidence intervals reported for all major point estimates? Is the confidence level—for example, 95%—stated, and is the same level of confidence used for all tables and throughout the paper?

☐ If statistical significance testing is used, are all probability level values correctly identified? Are asterisks attached to the appropriate table entries only when needed (as opposed to stating exact probabilities)? When used, is a probability level assigned the same number of asterisks in all tables in the same paper?

> ### ■ Table Checklist (continued)
>
> ☐ If all or part of a copyrighted table is reproduced or adapted, do the table notes give full credit to the copyright owner? Have you received written permission for reuse (in print and electronic form) from the copyright holder and sent a copy of that written permission to the journal editor with the final version of your paper?
>
> ☐ Is the table referred to in text?

Figures

5.20 Principles of Figure Use and Construction

There are many different types of figures; however, certain principles are the same for all figure types. First, consider the information value of the figure in the context of the paper in which it is to appear. If the figure does not add substantively to the understanding of the paper or duplicates other elements of the paper, it should not be included. Second, ask whether a figure is the best way to communicate the information. In some cases (particularly when quantitative information is being conveyed), a table may offer more precision than, say, a graph. Third, consider whether the figure can be produced in a way that captures the essential information without visually distracting detail. When considering inclusion of a figure, always remember that the information value of the figure must dominate other decisions. If you focus on the principle of information value, other questions—for example, use of color, use of photographic images, or magnitude of cropping of a picture—should be relatively easy to resolve.

You may wish to consider placing some figures in online supplemental archives when those are available. Figures placed in online supplemental archives are those that would enrich but are not essential to the basic understanding of the article. See section 6.04 for a detailed discussion of supplemental materials.

5.21 Types of Figures

Many types of figures can be used to present data to the reader. Sometimes the choice of which type to use will be obvious; at other times it will not. The more common types of figures used are described next.

- *Graphs* typically display the relationship between two quantitative indices or between a continuous quantitative variable (usually displayed as the y-axis) and groups of subjects displayed along the x-axis.
- *Charts* generally display nonquantitative information such as the flow of subjects through a process, for example, flow charts.
- *Maps* generally display spatial information.
- *Drawings* show information pictorially.
- *Photographs* contain direct visual representations of information.

Although these are general prototypes, there are many variations and versions of each, and the distinctions among many of them are not clear. Computer-generated images can be made to seem as if they are life-reflecting photographs, and photographs can be engineered to look more like drawings. Whenever photographic images are changed in a way that their basic information is modified, you must disclose the manipulation (see section 5.29).

Figures can be effectively used to illustrate complex theoretical formulations (see Figure 5.1) or to represent a theory graphically through a set of path models (see Figure 5.2). They can also show the sampling and flow of subjects through a randomized clinical trial or other experiment (see Figure 5.3) or the flow of participants in a survey study (see Figure 5.4). Figures can be used to illustrate the results of a one-way design with error bars representing precision of the resulting estimates (see Figure 5.5) or empirical results from a complex multi-

Figure 5.1. Complex Theoretical Formulations

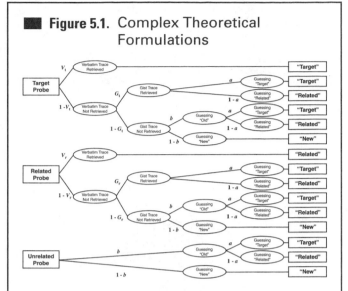

Figure X. Processing tree model for the simplified conjoint recognition paradigm. Rectangles on the left denote probe type, rectangles on the right denote responses. They are connected by branches of the processing tree that represent the combination of cognitive processes postulated by the model. V_t = probability of retrieving a target's verbatim trace given a target probe; V_r = probability of retrieving a target's verbatim trace given a related probe; G_t = probability of retrieving a target's gist trace given a target probe; G_r = probability of retrieving a target's gist trace given a related probe; b = probability of guessing that an item is either a target or a related probe; a = probability of guessing "target." Adapted from "A Simplified Conjoint Recognition Paradigm for the Measurement of Gist and Verbatim Memory," by C. Stahl and K. C. Klauer, 2008, *Journal of Experimental Psychology: Learning, Memory, and Cognition, 34,* p. 573. Copyright 2008 by the American Psychological Association.

variate model (see Figure 5.6). They can also show details concerning the kinds of responses being gathered and scoring methods (see Figure 5.7) as well as details of an experimental laboratory set-up (see Figure 5.8) and an experimental procedure (see Figure 5.9).

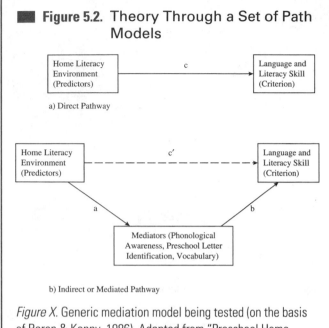

Figure 5.2. Theory Through a Set of Path Models

Figure X. Generic mediation model being tested (on the basis of Baron & Kenny, 1986). Adapted from "Preschool Home Literacy Practices and Children's Literacy Development: A Longitudinal Analysis," by M. Hood, E. Conlon, and G. Andrews, 2008, *Journal of Educational Psychology, 100,* p. 259. Copyright 2008 by the American Psychological Association.

5.22 Standards for Figures

The standards for good figures are simplicity, clarity, continuity, and (of course) information value.

A good figure

- augments rather than duplicates the text,
- conveys only essential facts,
- omits visually distracting detail,
- is easy to read—its elements (type, lines, labels, symbols, etc.) are large enough to be read with ease,
- is easy to understand—its purpose is readily apparent,
- is consistent with and in the same style as similar figures in the same article, and
- is carefully planned and prepared.

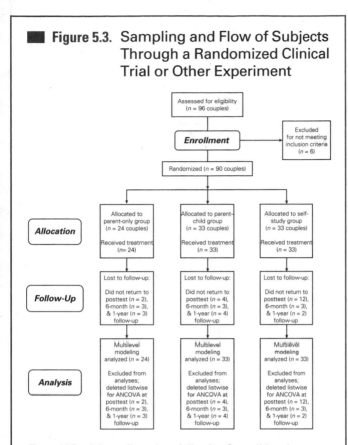

Figure 5.3. Sampling and Flow of Subjects Through a Randomized Clinical Trial or Other Experiment

Figure X. Participant flow chart following Consolidated Standards of Reporting Trials guidelines. ANCOVA = analysis of covariance. Adapted from "Evaluating a Brief Prevention Program for Improving Marital Conflict in Community Families," by E. M. Cummings, W. B. Faircloth, P. M. Mitchell, J. S. Cummings, and A. C. Schermerhorn, 2008, *Journal of Family Psychology, 22,* p. 196. Copyright 2008 by the American Psychological Association.

Be certain in figures of all types that

- lines are smooth and sharp,
- typeface is simple (sans serif) and legible,
- units of measure are provided,
- axes are clearly labeled, and

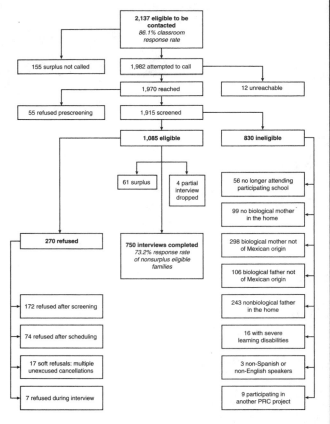

Figure 5.4. Flow of Participants in a Survey Study

Figure X. Response rate throughout the recruitment and interviewing processes. PRC = Prevention Research Center. Adapted from "Sampling and Recruitment in Studies of Cultural Influences on Adjustment: A Case Study With Mexican Americans," by M. W. Roosa, F. F. Liu, M. Torres, N. A. Gonzales, G. P. Knight, and D. Saenz, 2008, *Journal of Family Psychology, 22,* p. 299. Copyright 2008 by the American Psychological Association.

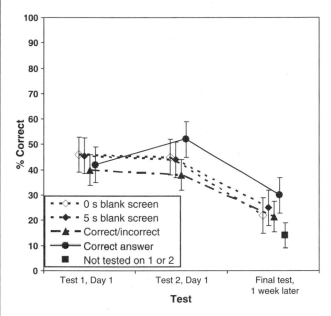

Figure 5.5. Results of One-Way Design Using Error Bars to Represent Precision of the Resulting Estimates

Figure X. Accuracy in Experiment 1 for each type of feedback and for each test. Error bars represent standard errors. Points are offset horizontally so that error bars are visible. Adapted from "When Does Feedback Facilitate Learning of Words?" by H. Pashler, N. J. Cepeda, J. T. Wixted, and D. Rohrer, 2005, *Journal of Experimental Psychology: Learning, Memory, and Cognition, 31,* p. 5. Copyright 2005 by the American Psychological Association.

■ elements within the figure are labeled or explained.

Be certain, for instance, to distinguish between error bars and confidence intervals. When using confidence intervals, clearly specify the size of the interval (e.g., 95%); when using error bars, provide the label for the error (e.g., standard error of the mean). In addition, be sure in all figures that

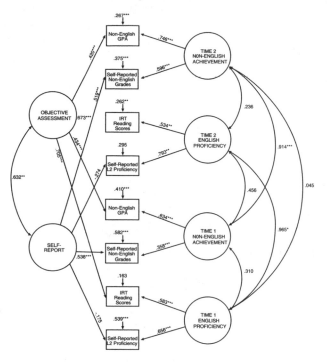

Figure 5.6. Empirical Results From a Complex Multivariate Model

Figure X. Multitrait–multimethod confirmatory factor analysis model of two correlated traits and two correlated methods across two measurement waves. Completely standardized robust maximum likelihood parameter estimates. The residual variance components (error variances) indicate the amount of unexplained variance. Thus, for each observed variable, $R^2 = (1 - \text{error variance})$. GPA = grade point average; IRT = item response theory; L2 = English. Adapted from "Native Language Proficiency, English Literacy, Academic Achievement, and Occupational Attainment in Limited-English-Proficient Students: A Latent Growth Modeling Perspective," by R. S. Guglielmi, 2008, *Journal of Educational Psychology, 100,* p. 329. Copyright 2008 by the American Psychological Association. $^*p < .05.$ $^{**}p < .01.$ $^{***}p < .001.$

Figure 5.7. Kinds of Responses Being Gathered and Scoring Methods

Figure X. Drawing copy task with elephant by smaller deletion cases (Cases 1, 2, and 3) and age and IQ-matched full deletion William syndrome cases. Adapted from "Williams Syndrome Deficits in Visual Spatial Processing Linked to GTF2IRD1 and GTF2I on Chromosome 7q11.23," by H. Hirota, R. Matsuoka, X.-N. Chen, L. S. Salandanan, A. Lincoln, F. E. Rose, . . . J. R. Korenberg, 2003, *Genetics in Medicine, 5,* p. 318. Copyright 2003 by American College of Medical Genetics. Reprinted with permission.

■ Figure 5.8. Details of an Experimental Laboratory Set-Up

a.

b.

Figure X. Schematic drawings of a bird's eye view of the table (a) and the test phase of the choice task (b). Numbers represent the dimensions in centimeters. Adapted from "Visual Experience Enhances Infants' Use of Task-Relevant Information in an Action Task," by S.-h. Wang and L. Kohne, 2007, *Developmental Psychology, 43,* p. 1515. Copyright 2003 by the American Psychological Association.

- sufficient information is given in the legend to make the figure understandable on its own,
- symbols are easy to differentiate, and
- the graphic is large enough for its elements to be discernible.

In general, high-quality graphics software handles the technical aspects of constructing figures. However, do examine the resulting images to ensure that figure guidelines have been followed and make any adjustments that might be needed.

■ Figure 5.9. Details of Experimental Procedure

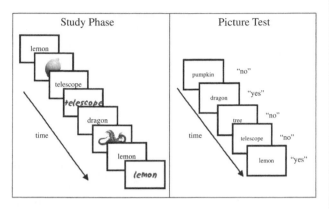

Figure X. Schematic of the criterial recollection task. At study, each black word was followed by the same word in red letters (depicted in italics) or by a colored picture. Black words were used at test as retrieval cues, under various retrieval instructions (picture test shown, with correct responses in quotes). Adapted from "Retrieval Monitoring and Anosognosia in Alzheimer's Disease," by D. A. Gallo, J. M. Chen, A. L. Wiseman, D. L. Schacter, and A. E. Budson, 2007, *Neuropsychology, 21,* p. 560. Copyright 2007 by the American Psychological Association.

5.23 Figure Legends and Captions

A *legend* explains the symbols used in the figure; it is placed within the figure. A *caption* is a concise explanation of the figure that is placed directly below the figure and serves as the title of the figure.

Legends. The legend is an integral part of the figure; therefore, it should have the same kind and proportion of lettering that appear in the rest of the figure. Capitalize major words in the legend.

Captions. The caption serves both as an explanation of the figure and as a figure title; therefore, the figure itself should not include a title. The caption should be a brief but descriptive phrase. Compare the following captions.

Too brief:

> *Figure 3.* Fixation duration.

Sufficiently descriptive:

> *Figure 3.* Fixation duration as a function of the delay between the beginning of eye fixation and the onset of the stimulus in Experiment 1.

After the descriptive phrase, add any information needed to clarify the figure: A reader should not have to refer to the text to decipher the figure's message. Always explain units of measurement, symbols, and abbreviations that are not included in the legend. If your graph includes error bars, explain whether they represent standard deviations, standard errors, confidence limits, or ranges; it is also helpful to display sample sizes. If statistically significant values are marked in the figure, explain the probability in the caption (follow the same system used for table notes; see section 5.16). Include within the caption any acknowledgment that a figure is reproduced from another source.

Make certain that the symbols, abbreviations, and terminology in the caption and legend agree with the symbols, abbreviations, and terminology in the figure, in other figures in the article, and in the text.

5.24 Planning Figures

When planning a figure, consider the following guidelines:

■ Parallel figures or figures of equal importance should be of equal size and scale.

■ Like figures should be combined to facilitate comparisons between them. For example, two figures can be placed one above the other and treated as one figure. Two line graphs with identical axes might be combined horizontally and treated as one figure.

■ A figure legend should be positioned within the borders of the figure (see Figure 5.5). Place labels for parts of a figure as close as possible to the components being identified.

5.25 Preparation of Figures

Figures intended for publication in scholarly journals should be computer generated using professional-level graphic software. Always check the file type requirements of the publisher to which you intend to submit your paper. Figures should be prepared at a resolution sufficient to produce high-quality images; appropriate resolution depends on figure type. Photographs (see section 5.29), for example, can be reproduced clearly at lower resolution than that needed for line art.

Image dimensions should be such that files can be easily transferred electronically. Avoid the use of three-dimensional and other effects (including color), except in rare instances in which they demonstrably enhance the presentation of your data. Individual publishers have stated policies with regard to color printing.

Size and proportion of elements. Each element must be large enough and sharp enough to be legible. Use a simple typeface (such as Arial, Futura, or Helvetica) with enough space between letters to avoid crowding. Letters should be clear, sharp, and uniformly dark and should be sized consistently throughout the figure. Type style affects legibility. For example, boldface type tends to thicken and become less readable. The size of lettering should be no smaller than 8 points and no larger than 14 points. As a general guideline, plot symbols should be about the size of a lowercase letter of an average label within the figure. Also consider the *weight* (i.e., size, density) of each element in a figure in relation to that of every other element, making the most important elements the most prominent. For example, curves on line graphs and outlines of bars on bar graphs should be bolder than axis labels, which should be bolder than the axes and tick marks.

Shading. Limit the number of different shadings used in a single graphic. If different shadings are used to distinguish bars or segments of a graph, choose shadings that are distinct (e.g., the best option to distinguish two sets of bars is no shading [open] and black [solid]). If more than three shadings are required, a table may be a better presentation of the data. Use computer-generated art in such a way as to maximize the clarity of the resulting graphic. And as always, keep it simple and clean looking.

Presenting Electrophysiological, Radiological, and Other Biological Data

Electrophysiological and radiological data present special challenges because the data are complex and no single convention exists for presenting these types of data. The lack of a single, well-established standard requires that labeling of all aspects of the presentation be done clearly and completely (readers are referred to Devlin & Poldrack, 2007; Mildenberger, Eichenberg, & Martin, 2002; Picton et al., 2000; see also http://www.fmrimethods.org). Do not assume that readers will know the convention that you are following. Most graphical and image-based representations of the basic data are highly processed, edited, and enhanced. The high level of processing of these forms of data makes it essential that the processing methods are clearly identified and that enhanced data (and the ensuing representation of such enhanced data) are clearly and openly identified.

In selecting data elements to present in the print version of the document, focus first on principles of clarity of representation, necessity for understanding, and coherence among representations. With the availability of online supplemental archives, carefully consider the readability of the text when deciding whether to include complex graphs and images in the text proper. When materials are better viewed in nonprint media or when images and graphics contain more information than can easily be comprehended in the usual print formats—for example, those that are greatly enhanced through the use of color or instances in which numerous images are needed to communicate the essential features of the study—consider the use of online supplemental archives for the presentation of the bulk of this information.

Many procedures used for the display of biologically related data use color, motion, or other display features not best rendered in black-and-white printing. In particular, fMRI images are typically coded in color, where color differences indicate activation differences. In the genetics area, gene staining results are often presented in color. Dynamical spread of brain activation can be displayed through color video clips. In the material that follows, we present print examples that are appropriate for black-and-white printing but also point to a number of examples (particularly those using color) that are included on the website (see www.apastyle.org) accompanying the sixth edition of the *Publication Manual of the American Psychological Association* (APA, 2010).

5.26 Electrophysiological Data

When presenting electrophysiological data, clear labeling is essential; for example, in the presentation of event-related brain potential data, it is essential that the direction of negativity (i.e., negative up or down) be indicated as well as the scale of the response. Information that is necessary for proper interpretation of the graphic, such as number or placement of electrodes, should accompany the graphic display. The graphic image and the points made in the text should be closely allied. Eliminate extraneous materials from graphic presentation (see Figure 5.10).

5.27 Radiological (Imaging) Data

When presenting brain images, clearly label each image. When axial or coronal sections are being displayed, clearly label which hemisphere is the left and which the right. When saggital slices are displayed, clearly indicate whether each slice is of the right or the left hemisphere. When slices are shown, show also an image that indicates where the slices were taken to help orient the reader. Specify the coordinate space in which the images have been normalized (e.g., Talairach, MNI).

Cutaway views of the brain that show activations interior to it can be useful if the cutaways clearly depict the

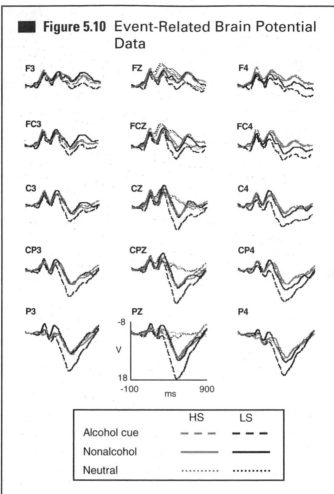

Figure 5.10 Event-Related Brain Potential Data

Figure X. Event-related brain potential waveforms elicited by alcoholic and nonalcoholic beverage cues as a function of sensitivity group. Waveforms elicited by frequent neutral (nontarget) images are presented for midline locations to illustrate the oddball effect in these data. Stimulus onset occurred at 0 ms. Electrodes are arrayed from most anterior (top) to most posterior (bottom) and from left to right as they were positioned on the scalp. HS = high alcohol sensitivity group; LS = low alcohol sensitivity group. Adapted from "Effects of Alcohol Sensitivity on P3 Event-Related Potential Reactivity to Alcohol Cues," by B. D. Bartholow, E. A. Henry, and S. A. Lust, 2007, *Psychology of Addictive Behaviors, 21,* p. 560. Copyright 2007 by the American Psychological Association.

tissue that has been excised. When activations are super-imposed on a surface-rendered image of a brain, include a clear explanation of what activations are being shown, particularly with regard to the depth of the activation that has been brought to the surface; the use of flattened surface images may help make the data clearer. When using color, use it consistently in all representations within the document and clearly specify the color–scale mapping (see www.apastyle.org).

Neuroimaging data almost always require extensive postacquisition processing. Details of the processing methods should accompany their display (see Figure 5.11).

■ **Figure 5.11.** Neuroimaging Data With Details of Processing Information

Figure X. Lesion maps for the two right hemisphere patients plotted onto a normal template brain using MRIcro software (Rorden & Brett, 2000). Affected regions (translucent white) are plotted onto axial slices, with numbers above each slice indicating *Z* coordinates in Talairach space. Adapted from "Central Perceptual Load Does Not Reduce Ipsilesional Flanker Interference in Parietal Extinction," by J. C. Snow and J. B. Mattingley, 2008, *Neuropsychology, 22,* p. 375. Copyright 2008 by the American Psychological Association.

Photomicrographs are often used in cell-staining and other types of imaging studies. When preparing photomicrographs, include a scale bar and staining materials information in the figure caption.

5.28 Genetic Data

As with other displays of biological material, clear labeling enhances the display of genetic information such as deletion patterns—be they of the physical map variety (see Figure 5.12) or the photographic stain variety (see example at www.apastyle.org). Present information concerning locations, distances, markers, and identification methods with the figure. Genetic data displays often contain much information; careful editing of the image, and of its legend, can improve the communicative value of the figure.

5.29 Photographs

Photographic images are almost always submitted as digital files embedded in or attached to the electronic version of the manuscript. It is essential that these images be submitted at appropriate levels of resolution.

Figure X. (facing page) Physical map of the common Williams syndrome deletion. Genes mapping in this region are represented by black boxes (names reading vertically). Bacterial artificial chromosomes, P1-derived artificial chromosomes, and cosmid clones spanning this region are indicated below the genes and are described in the Method section. The black horizontal lines depict the approximate size and extent of deletions in the three cases with atypical deletions and in typical subjects with Williams syndrome. Adapted from "Williams Syndrome Deficits in Visual Spatial Processing Linked to GTF2IRD1 and GTF2I on Chromosome 7q11.23," by H. Hirota, R. Matsuoka, X.-N. Chen, L. S. Salandanan, A. Lincoln, F. E. Rose, . . . J. R. Korenberg, 2003, *Genetics in Medicine, 5,* p. 315. Copyright 2003 by American College of Medical Genetics. Reprinted with permission.

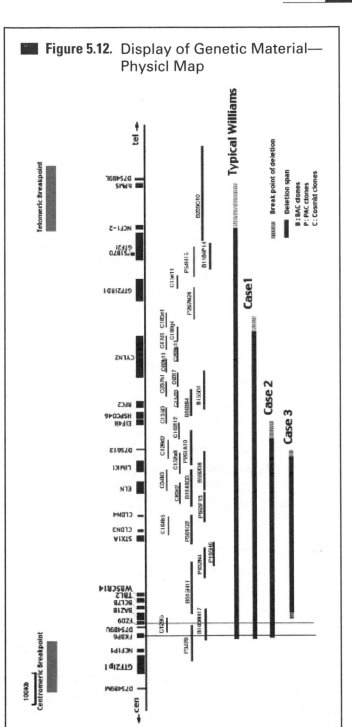

Figure 5.12. Display of Genetic Material—Physicl Map

Because reproduction softens contrast and detail in photographs, starting with rich contrast and sharp prints will improve the final print version of the image. The camera view and the lighting should highlight the subject and provide high contrast; a light or dark background can provide even more contrast.

Photographs must be of professional quality and should be presented as black-and-white images, unless they include color-specific information relevant to the study (e.g., differently colored stimuli). Submit the image as a file type appropriate to the needs of the publication to which you are submitting. Do not submit color image files for figures intended for black-and-white printing; the transition from color to black and white for reproduction is unpredictable and can result in misleading images. It is the author's responsibility to ensure that the final representation is accurate. If color photos are necessary, consult your publication's instructions to authors for guidelines regarding color images.

Photographs usually benefit from cropping (i.e., eliminating what is not to be reproduced), just as careful editing of words can produce a more comprehensible text. Cropping recomposes the photo, eliminates extraneous detail, and centers the image. Before cropping, ensure that the image is straight (e.g., that vertical lines are truly vertical); use your software application to align the image if necessary. When used appropriately, these alterations can enhance and clarify the image and make it more useful as a means of scientific communication; they also help to protect the identity of individuals. However, the same technology can be used to deceive. Ethical principles of publication forbid any intentional misrepresentation of images in exactly the same way that fraudulent data manipulation is forbidden. When an image that might reasonably be thought to be a photographic image (as opposed to an image that is clearly a constructed image—a table, chart cartoon, etc.) has been altered in a manner beyond simple cropping, clearly indicate in a note that accompanies the image that it has been altered.

If you photograph a person, obtain a signed release from that person to use the photograph. If you use a photograph from another source, try to obtain the original photograph because photographs of photographs do not print clearly. Obtain written permission for reuse (in both print and electronic form) from the copyright holder, and acknowledge the author and the copyright holder in the figure caption (see sections 5.06 and 5.23). You may need to obtain permission from the photographer as well because professional photographs do not meet all the criteria of work for hire and are usually the property of the photographer.

5.30 Figure Checklist

The following checklist may be helpful in ensuring that your figure communicates most effectively and conforms to APA Style and formatting conventions.

▨ Figure Checklist

☐ Is the figure necessary?

☐ Is the figure simple, clear, and free of extraneous detail?

☐ Is the figure title descriptive of the content of the figure?

☐ Are all elements of the figure clearly labeled?

☐ Are the magnitude, scale, and direction of grid elements clearly labeled?

☐ Are figures of equally important concepts prepared according to the same scale?

☐ Are all figures numbered consecutively with Arabic numerals?

☐ Are all figures mentioned in the text?

☐ Has written permission for print and electronic reuse been obtained? Is proper credit given in the figure caption?

☐ Have all substantive modifications to photographic images been disclosed?

☐ Are the figures being submitted in a file format acceptable to the publisher?

☐ Have the files been produced at a sufficiently high resolution to allow for accurate reproduction?

6

Footnotes, Appendices, and Supplemental Material

In this chapter, we describe the manuscript elements typically used to support the argument—footnotes, appendices, and supplemental materials. Although these elements contain information that may not be essential to the immediate theme of the article, they are used to support and enrich the reader's understanding.

Footnotes

6.01 Use of Footnotes

Footnotes are used to provide additional content or to acknowledge copyright permission status.

Content footnotes. Content footnotes supplement or amplify substantive information in the text; they should not include complicated, irrelevant, or nonessential information. Because they can be distracting to readers, such footnotes should be included only if they strengthen the discussion. A content footnote should convey just one idea; if you find yourself creating paragraphs or displaying equations as you are writing a footnote, then the main text or an appendix probably would be a more suitable place to present your information. Another alternative is to indicate in a short footnote that the material is available online as supplemental material. In most cases, an author integrates an article best by presenting important information in the text, not in a footnote.

Copyright permission footnotes. Copyright permission footnotes acknowledge the source of lengthy quotations, scale and test items, and figures and tables that have been reprinted or adapted. Authors must obtain permission to reproduce or adapt material from a copyrighted source. (See Chapter 7 for a discussion of what authors should know about permissions and copyright.)

A numbered footnote is generally used to provide source material for long quotations. For tables, the source material is provided in a table note (see section 5.16), and for figures, the source is credited at the end of the caption (see section 5.23). Use the wording below for copyright permission footnotes.

Type of source	Copyright permission footnote
Journal	From [or The data in column 1 are from] "Title of Article," by A. N. Author and C. O. Author, year, *Title of Journal, Volume*, p. xx. Copyright [year] by the Name of Copyright Holder. Reprinted [or adapted] with permission.
Book	From [or The data in column 1 are from] *Title of Book* (p. xxx), by A. N. Author and C. O. Author, year, Place of Publication: Publisher. Copyright [year] by the Name of Copyright Holder. Reprinted [or adapted] with permission.

Number all footnotes consecutively in the order in which they appear in the manuscript with superscript

Arabic numerals. Footnote numbers should be super-scripted, like this,[1] following any punctuation mark except a dash. A footnote number that appears with a dash—like this[2]—always precedes the dash. (The number falls inside a closing parenthesis if it applies only to matter within the parentheses, like this.[3]) Do not place footnote numbers in text headings. Subsequent references to a footnote are by parenthetical note:

> the same results (see Footnote 3)

When using the footnote function in your word-processing program, place each content or copyright permission footnote at the bottom of the page on which it is discussed. Footnotes may alternatively be placed in consecutive order on a separate page after the references. Be sure that the number of the footnote corresponds with the appropriate text discussion.

6.02 Author Note

An author note appears with each printed article to identify each author's departmental affiliation, provide acknowledgments, state any disclaimers or perceived conflict of interest, and provide a point of contact for the interested reader. (Students should note that an author note is usually not a requirement for theses and dissertations.) Notes should be arranged as follows.

First paragraph: Complete departmental affiliation. Identify departmental affiliations at the time of the study for all authors. Format as follows: name of the author as it appears in the byline, comma, department name, comma, university name, semicolon, next author name, and so on, and end with a period. If an author is not affiliated with an institution, provide the city and state (provide city and country for authors whose affiliations are outside of the United States, and include province for authors in Canada or Australia). No degrees should be given, and state names should be spelled out.

Second paragraph: Changes of affiliation (if any). Identify any changes in author affiliation subsequent to the time of the study. Use the following wording: [author's name] is now at [affiliation]. The affiliation should include the department and institution.

Third paragraph.

  Acknowledgments. Identify grants or other financial support (and the source, if appropriate) for your study; do not precede grant numbers by No. or #. Next, acknowledge colleagues who assisted in conducting the study or critiquing the manuscript. Do not acknowledge the persons routinely involved in the review and acceptance of manuscripts—peer reviewers or editors, associate editors, and consulting editors of the journal in which the article is to appear. (If you would like to acknowledge a specific idea raised by a reviewer, do so in the text where the idea is discussed.) In this paragraph, also explain any special agreements concerning authorship, such as if authors contributed equally to the study. End this paragraph with thanks for personal assistance, such as in manuscript preparation.

  Special circumstances. If there are any special circumstances, disclose them before the acknowledgments in the third paragraph. For example, if the manuscript is based on data also used in a previously published report (e.g., a longitudinal study) or a doctoral dissertation, state that information in this paragraph. Also, acknowledge the publication of related reports (e.g., reports on the same database). If any relationships may be perceived as a conflict of interest (e.g., if you own stock in a company that manufactures a drug used in your study), explain them here. (For additional information on conflict of interest and publication ethics, see the *Publication Manual of the American Psychological Association,* 2010, Chapter 1.) If your employer or granting organization requires a disclaimer stating, for example, that the research reported does not reflect the views of that organization, such a statement is included in this paragraph.

Fourth paragraph: Person to contact (mailing address, e-mail). Provide a complete mailing address for correspondence. End this paragraph with an e-mail address and no period.

Jane Doe, Department of Psychology, University of Illinois at Urbana–Champaign; John Smith, Department of Educational Psychology, University of Chicago.

John Smith is now at Department of Psychology, University of California, San Diego.

This research was supported in part by grants from the National Institute on Aging and from the John D. and Catherine T. MacArthur Foundation.

Correspondence concerning this article should be addressed to Jane Doe, Department of Psychology, University of Illinois, Champaign, IL 61820. E-mail: jdoe@uiuc.edu

Place the author note on the title page, below the title, byline, and affiliation. Center the label *Author Note*. Start each paragraph of the note with an indent. The author note is not numbered or cited in the text.

Appendices and Supplemental Materials

Sometimes, material that supplements article content would be distracting or inappropriate in the body of the manuscript. Material of this type can be included in an appendix or in a supplemental materials section—the former being an element of the print version of the article, the latter being an online supplemental archive that the publisher of the journal maintains.

6.03 Appendices

An appendix is appropriate for materials that are relatively brief and that are easily presented in print format. Some examples of material suitable for an appendix are (a) a list of stimulus materials (e.g., those used in psycholinguistic research), (b) a detailed description of a complex piece of equipment, (c) a list of articles that provided the source data for a meta-analysis but are not directly referred to in any other way in an article, and (d) a detailed demographic description of subpopulations in the study and other detailed and/or complex reporting items suggested in the reporting standards section of this chapter.

If your manuscript has only one appendix, label it *Appendix*; if your manuscript has more than one appendix, label each one with a capital letter (*Appendix A*, *Appendix B*, etc.) in the order in which it is mentioned in the main text. Each appendix must have a title. In the text, refer to appendices by their labels:

> produced the same results for both studies (see Appendices A and B for complete proofs).

Like the main text, an appendix may include headings and subheadings as well as tables, figures, and displayed equations. Number each appendix table and figure, and number displayed equations if necessary for later reference; precede the number with the letter of the appendix in which it is included (e.g., Table A1). In a sole appendix, which is not labeled with a letter, precede all tables, figures, and equation numbers with the letter *A* to distinguish them from those of the main text. All appendix tables and figures must be cited within the appendix and numbered in order of citation.

If one table constitutes an entire appendix, the centered appendix label and title serve in lieu of a table number and title. Generally, treat multiple tables as separate appendices. If multiple tables (but no text) are combined into one appendix, number the tables.

Begin each appendix on a separate page. Center the word *Appendix* and the identifying capital letters (*A*, *B*, etc., in the order in which they are mentioned in text) at the top of the page. Center the title of the appendix, and use uppercase and lowercase letters. Begin the text of the appendix flush left, followed by indented paragraphs.

6.04 Supplemental Materials

Web-based, online supplemental archives tend to be more appropriate for material that is more useful when available as a direct download as well as materials that are not easily presented in standard print format. Some examples of materials suitable for inclusion in online supplemental archives are (a) lengthy computer code, (b) details of mathematical or computational models, (c) audio or video clips, (d) oversized tables, (e) detailed intervention protocols, (f) primary or supplementary data sets, (g) expanded methodology sections, and (h) color figures. Because this content may be useful to the field, APA and many other publishers make it possible to provide them to a wide audience by posting them on the web, with a link to the published article. These files (like an appendix) then become part of the primary journal record and cannot be augmented, altered, or deleted.

Materials for inclusion in supplemental online archives should be submitted in formats that will be widely accessible. The following multimedia formats are generally widely available to most users and are preferred:

- Text—ASCII, Word, PDF, HTML
- Tables—Excel, Word, HTML, XHTML, XML
- Audio and Video—AVI, MPG, Quicktime, RM, MP3, WAV
- Animation—GIF, JPEG, Flash/Shockwave
- Images—GIF, JPEG, TIFF

Less widely used file formats, including TeX, LaTeX, any client- or server-side scripting (e.g., Java, CGI), executable files, and software applications, are acceptable but may be of less use to the reader who does not have access to specialized programs. Many users refuse to deal with executable files or operate from systems that refuse to access them.

For APA journals, the link to online supplemental archives that appears in the published article leads readers to a landing page that includes a bibliographic citation, a link to the published article, and a context statement and link for each supplemental material file (see an example of a sample landing page at www.apastyle.org). Supplemental materials should include enough information to make their contents interpretable when accompanied by the published text.

Most journals make supplemental materials subject to peer review and require that they be submitted with the initial manuscript. Once accepted, the supplemental materials will be posted with no further editing or polishing.

Include an appendix or supplemental materials only if they help readers to understand, evaluate, or replicate the study or theoretical argument being made. Be sure that such materials meet copyright standards, represent the data accurately, and account for confidentiality and the protection of human subjects (e.g., content of video clips if human images). Be sure that all relevant ethical standards have been followed for appendices and supplemental materials.

7

Crediting Sources

In this chapter, we provide the ground rules for acknowledging how others contributed to your work. We begin by describing the appropriate level of citation and offer a brief review of plagiarism and self-plagiarism. Next, we offer guidelines on formatting quoted material in text and information on seeking permission to reprint or adapt previously published material. This is followed by instruction on citing sources in text and a description of key elements of the reference list.

When to Cite

Cite the work of those individuals whose ideas, theories, or research have directly influenced your work. They may provide key background information, support or dispute your thesis, or offer critical definitions and data. Citation of an article implies that you have personally read the cited work. In addition to crediting the ideas of others that you used to build your thesis, provide documentation for all facts and figures that are not common knowledge. Figure 7.1 provides an example of the appro-

Figure 7.1. Example of Appropriate Citation Level

Left-handers make up 8% to 13% of most human populations, with left-handedness more common in men than in women (Gilbert & Wysocki, 1992; McManus, 1991). Secondary school and university students engaged in "interactive" sports such as tennis and basketball are significantly more likely to be left-handed than those engaged in "noninteractive" sports such as swimming or rowing, or than those in the general population (Grouios, Tsorbatzoudis, Alexandris, & Barkoukis, 2000; Raymond et al., 1996). One possible explanation for this handedness bias is that left-handers are better than right-handers at some visuomotor tasks, as has been invoked to explain the left-handed bias among elite tennis players (Holtzen, 2000).

Note. Adapted from "Frequency-Dependent Performance and Handedness in Professional Baseball Players (*Homo sapiens*)," by E. D. Clotfelter, 2008, *Journal of Comparative Psychology, 122,* p. 68. Copyright 2008 by the American Psychological Association.

priate level of citation, adapted from an article in an APA journal.

The number of sources you cite in your work will vary by the intent of the article. For most articles, aim to cite one or two of the most representative sources for each key point. However, because the intent of a review article is to acquaint readers with all that has been written on a topic, authors of literature reviews typically include a more exhaustive list of citations.

7.01 Plagiarism

As stated in the *Publication Manual of the American Psychological Association* (APA, 2010), "Authors do not present the work of another as if it were their own work" (p. 16). Whether paraphrasing, quoting an author directly, or describing an idea that influenced your work, you must credit the source. To avoid charges of plagiarism, take careful notes as you research to keep track of your sources and cite those sources according to the guidelines presented in this chapter.

7.02 Self-Plagiarism

Whereas *plagiarism* refers to the practice of claiming credit for the words, ideas, and concepts of others, *self-plagiarism* refers to the practice of presenting one's own previously published work as though it were new. As noted in Chapter 1 of the *Publication Manual* (APA, 2010), "the core of the new document must constitute an original contribution to knowledge, and only the amount of previously published material necessary to understand that contribution should be included, primarily in the discussion of theory and methodology" (p. 16). Avoid charges of self-plagiarism by familiarizing yourself with ethical standards regarding duplicate publication and legal standards of fair use.

Quoting and Paraphrasing

7.03 Direct Quotation of Sources

Reproduce word for word material directly quoted from another author's work or from your own previously published work, material replicated from a test item, and verbatim instructions to participants. When quoting, always provide the author, year, and specific page citation or paragraph number for nonpaginated material (see section 7.05) in the text and include a complete reference in the reference list (see section 7.11 for exceptions to this rule).

If the quotation comprises fewer than 40 words, incorporate it into text and enclose the quotation with double quotation marks. If the quotation appears in midsentence, end the passage with quotation marks, cite the source in parentheses immediately after the quotation marks, and continue the sentence. Use no other punctuation unless the meaning of the sentence requires such punctuation.

> Interpreting these results, Robbins et al. (2003) suggested that the "therapists in dropout cases may have inadvertently validated parental negativity about the adolescent without adequately responding to the adolescent's needs or concerns" (p. 541), contributing to an overall climate of negativity.

If the quotation appears at the end of a sentence, close the quoted passage with quotation marks, cite the source in parentheses immediately after the quotation marks, and end with a period or other punctuation outside the final parenthesis.

> Confusing this issue is the overlapping nature of roles in palliative care, whereby "medical needs are met by those in the medical disciplines; non-medical needs may be addressed by anyone on the team" (Csikai & Chaitin, 2006, p. 112).

If the quotation comprises 40 or more words, display it in a freestanding block of text and omit the quotation marks. Start such a *block quotation* on a new line and indent the block about a half inch from the left margin (in the same position as a new paragraph). If there are additional paragraphs within the quotation, indent the first line of each an additional half inch. Double-space the entire quotation. At the end of a block quotation, cite the quoted source and the page or paragraph number in parentheses after the final punctuation mark.

> Others have contradicted this view:
>
> > Co-presence does not ensure intimate interaction among all group members. Consider large-scale social gatherings in which hundreds or thousands of people gather in a location to perform a ritual or celebrate an event.
> >
> > In these instances, participants are able to see the visible manifestation of the group, the physical gathering, yet their ability to make direct, intimate connections with those around them is limited by the sheer magnitude of the assembly. (Purcell, 1997, pp. 111–112)

Alternatively, if the quoted source is cited in the sentence introducing the block quote (e.g., "In 1997, Purcell contradicted this view. . . "), only the page or paragraph number is needed at the end of the quotation.

7.04 Paraphrasing Material

When paraphrasing or referring to an idea contained in another work, you are encouraged to provide a page or paragraph number, especially when it would help an interested reader locate the relevant passage in a long or complex text.

7.05 Direct Quotations of Online Material Without Pagination

Credit direct quotations of online material by giving the author, year, and page number in parentheses. Many electronic sources do not provide page numbers. If paragraph numbers are visible, use them in place of page numbers. Use the abbreviation *para.*

> Basu and Jones (2007) went so far as to suggest the need for a new "intellectual framework in which to consider the nature and form of regulation in cyberspace" (para. 4).

If the document includes headings and neither paragraph nor page numbers are visible, cite the heading and the number of the paragraph following it to direct the reader to the location of the quoted material.

> In their study, Verbunt, Pernot, and Smeets (2008) found that "the level of perceived disability in patients with fibromyalgia seemed best explained by their mental health condition and less by their physical condition" (Discussion section, para. 1).

In some cases in which no page or paragraph numbers are visible, headings may be too unwieldy to cite in full. Instead, use a short title enclosed in quotation marks for the parenthetical citation:

> "Empirical studies have found mixed results on the efficacy of labels in educating consumers and

changing consumption behavior" (Golan, Kuchler, & Krissof, 2007, "Mandatory Labeling Has Targeted," para. 4).

(The heading was "Mandatory Labeling Has Targeted Information Gaps and Social Objectives.")

7.06 Accuracy of Quotations

Direct quotations must be accurate. Except as noted here and in sections 7.07 and 7.08, the quotation must follow the wording, spelling, and interior punctuation of the original source, even if the source is incorrect.

If any incorrect spelling, punctuation, or grammar in the source might confuse readers, insert the word *sic,* italicized and bracketed, immediately after the error in the quotation. (See sections 2.09 and 2.11 regarding the use of brackets in quotations.) Always check the manuscript copy against the source to ensure that there are no discrepancies.

7.07 Changes From the Source Requiring No Explanation

The first letter of the first word in a quotation may be changed to an uppercase or a lowercase letter. The punctuation mark at the end of a sentence may be changed to fit the syntax. Single quotation marks may be changed to double quotation marks and vice versa. Any other changes (e.g., italicizing words for emphasis or omitting words; see section 7.08) must be explicitly indicated.

7.08 Changes From the Source Requiring Explanation

Omitting material. Use three spaced ellipsis points (. . .) within a sentence to indicate that you have omitted material from the original source. Use four points to indicate any omission between two sentences. The first point indicates the period at the end of the first sentence quoted, and the three spaced ellipsis points follow. Do not use ellipsis points at the beginning or end of any quotation unless, to prevent misinterpretation, you need to emphasize that the quotation begins or ends in midsentence.

Inserting material. Use brackets, not parentheses, to enclose material such as an addition or explanation inserted in a quotation by some person other than the original author (see also the second example in section 2.11).

> "They are studying, from an evolutionary perspective, to what extent [children's] play is a luxury that can be dispensed with when there are too many other competing claims on the growing brain . . ." (Henig, 2008, p. 40).

Adding emphasis. If you want to emphasize a word or words in a quotation, italicize the word or words. Immediately after the italicized words, insert within brackets the words *emphasis added*, that is, [emphasis added] (see section 2.09, second example).

7.09 Citations Within Quotations

Do not omit citations embedded within the original material you are quoting. The works cited need not be included in the list of references (unless you happen to cite them as primary sources elsewhere in your paper).

> "In the United States, the American Cancer Society (2007) estimated that about 1 million cases of NMSC and 59,940 cases of melanoma would be diagnosed in 2007, with melanoma resulting in 8,110 deaths" (Miller et al., 2009, p. 209).

7.10 Permission to Quote, Reprint, or Adapt

You may need written permission from the owner of copyrighted work if you include lengthy quotations or if you include reprinted or adapted tables, figures, questionnaires, or test items (see the cautionary note in section 5.06).

Reprinting indicates that the material is reproduced exactly as it appeared originally, without modifications, in the way in which it was intended. *Adaptation* refers to the modification of material so that it is suitable for a new purpose (e.g., paraphrasing or presenting an original theory discussed in a long passage in a published article in a new way that suits your study; using part of a table or figure in a new table or figure in your manuscript). Requirements for obtaining permission to quote copyrighted material vary from one copyright owner to another; for example, APA policy permits authors to use, with some exceptions, a maximum of three figures or tables from a journal article or book chapter, single text extracts of fewer than 400 words, or a series of text extracts that total fewer than 800 words without requesting formal permission from APA. It is important to check with the publisher or copyright owner regarding specific requirements for permission to quote from or adapt copyrighted material.

It is the author's responsibility to find out whether permission is required from the copyright owner and to obtain it for both print and electronic reuse. APA cannot publish previously copyrighted material that exceeds the copyright holder's determination of "fair use" without permission.

If you must obtain written permission from the copyright owner, append a footnote to the quoted material with a superscript number, and in the footnote acknowledge permission from the owner of the copyright. Format the footnote as shown in section 6.01.

Citing References in Text

References in APA publications are cited in text with an author–date citation system and are listed alphabetically in the references list. This style of citation briefly identifies the source for readers and enables them to locate the source of information in the alphabetical reference list at the end of the article.

7.11 Agreement of Text and Reference List

Each reference cited in text must appear in the reference list, and each entry in the reference list must be cited in text. Make certain that each source referenced appears in both places and that the text citation and reference list entry are identical in spelling of author names and year.

However, two kinds of material are cited only in the text: references to classical works such as the Bible and the Qur'an, whose sections are standardized across editions, and references to personal communications (see sections 7.19 and 7.21). References in a meta-analysis are not cited in text unless they are also mentioned in the text (see section 7.27).

7.12 One Work by One Author

The author–date method of citation requires that the surname of the author (do not include suffixes such as *Jr.*) and the year of publication be inserted in the text at the appropriate point:

> Kessler (2003) found that among epidemiological samples

> Early onset results in a more persistent and severe course (Kessler, 2003).

If the name of the author appears as part of the narrative, as in the first example, cite only the year of publication in parentheses. Otherwise, place both the name and the year, separated by a comma, in parentheses (as in the second example). Even if the reference includes month and year, include only the year in the text citation. In the rare case in which both the year and the author are given as part of the textual discussion, do not add parenthetical information:

> In 2003, Kessler's study of epidemiological samples showed that

Within a paragraph, when the name of the author is part of the narrative (as in the first example above), you need not include the year in subsequent nonparenthetical references to a study as long as the study cannot be confused with other studies cited in the article. Do include the year in all parenthetical citations:

> Among epidemiological samples, Kessler (2003) found that early onset social anxiety disorder results in a more potent and severe course. Kessler also found. . . . The study also showed that there was a high rate of comorbidity with alcohol abuse or dependence and major depression (Kessler, 2003).

However, when both the name and the year are in parentheses (as in the second example above), include the year in subsequent citations within the paragraph:

> Early onset results in a more persistent and severe course (Kessler, 2003).

> Kessler (2003) also found. . . .

7.13 One Work by Multiple Authors

When a work has two authors, cite both names every time the reference occurs in text. When a work has three, four, or five authors, cite all authors the first time the reference occurs; in subsequent citations, include only the surname of the first author followed by *et al.* (not italicized and with a period after *al*) and the year if it is the first citation of the reference within a paragraph.

> Kisangau, Lyaruu, Hosea, and Joseph (2007) found [Use as first citation in text.]

> Kisangau et al. (2007) found [Use as subsequent first citation per paragraph thereafter.]

> Kisangau et al. found [Omit year from subsequent citations after first nonparenthetical citation within a paragraph. Include the year in sub-

sequent citations if first citation within a paragraph is parenthetical. See section 7.12.]

Exception: If two references of more than three surnames with the same year shorten to the same form (e.g., both Ireys, Chernoff, DeVet, & Kim, 2001, and Ireys, Chernoff, Stein, DeVet, & Silver, 2001, shorten to Ireys et al., 2001), cite the surnames of the first authors and of as many of the subsequent authors as necessary to distinguish the two references, followed by a comma and *et al.*

> Ireys, Chernoff, DeVet, et al. (2001) and Ireys, Chernoff, Stein, et al. (2001)

Precede the final name in a multiple-author citation in running text by the word *and*. In parenthetical material, in tables and captions, and in the reference list, join the names by an ampersand (&):

> as Kurtines and Szapocznik (2003) demonstrated

> as has been shown (Jöreskog & Sörbom, 2007)

When a work has six or more authors, cite only the surname of the first author followed by *et al.* (not italicized and with a period after *al*) and the year for the first and subsequent citations. (See section 7.28 and Example 2 in Chapter 8 for how to cite works with more than six authors in the reference list.) If two references with six or more authors shorten to the same form, cite the surnames of the first authors and of as many of the subsequent authors as necessary to distinguish the two references, followed by a comma and *et al.* For example, suppose you have entries for the following references:

> Kosslyn, Koenig, Barrett, Cave, Tang, and Gabrieli (1996)

> Kosslyn, Koenig, Gabrieli, Tang, Marsolek, and Daly (1996)

In text you would cite them, respectively, as

Kosslyn, Koenig, Barrett, et al. (1996) and
Kosslyn, Koenig, Gabrieli, et al. (1996)

Table 7.1 illustrates the basic citation styles. Exceptions and citation styles that do not work in the tabular format are discussed in text or included as part of the example references.

7.14 Groups as Authors

The names of groups that serve as authors (e.g., corporations, associations, government agencies, and study groups) are usually spelled out each time they appear in a text citation. The names of some group authors are spelled out in the first citation and abbreviated thereafter. In deciding whether to abbreviate the name of a group author, use the general rule that you need to give enough information in the text citation for the reader to locate the entry in the reference list without difficulty. If the name is long and cumbersome and if the abbreviation is familiar or readily understandable, you may abbreviate the name in the second and subsequent citations. If the name is short or if the abbreviation would not be readily understandable, write out the name each time it occurs (see examples in Table 7.1).

7.15 Authors With the Same Surname

If a reference list includes publications by two or more primary authors with the same surname, include the first author's initials in all text citations, even if the year of publication differs. Initials help the reader to avoid confusion within the text and to locate the entry in the list of references (see section 7.26 for the order of appearance in the reference list).

References:

Light, I. (2006). *Deflecting immigration: Networks, markets, and regulation in Los Angeles.* New York, NY: Russell Sage Foundation.

Table 7.1. Basic Citation Styles

Type of citation	First citation in text	Subsequent citations in text	Parenthetical format, first citation in text	Parenthetical format, subsequent citations in text
One work by one author	Walker (2007)	Walker (2007)	(Walker, 2007)	(Walker, 2007)
One work by two authors	Walker and Allen (2004)	Walker and Allen (2004)	(Walker & Allen, 2004)	(Walker & Allen, 2004)
One work by three authors	Bradley, Ramirez, and Soo (1999)	Bradley et al. (1999)	(Bradley, Ramirez, & Soo, 1999)	(Bradley et al., 1999)
One work by four authors	Bradley, Ramirez, Soo, and Walsh (2006)	Bradley et al. (2006)	(Bradley, Ramirez, Soo, & Walsh, 2006)	(Bradley et al., 2006)
One work by five authors	Walker, Allen, Bradley, Ramirez, and Soo (2008)	Walker et al. (2008)	(Walker, Allen, Bradley, Ramirez, & Soo, 2008)	(Walker et al., 2008)
One work by six or more authors	Wasserstein et al. (2005)	Wasserstein et al. (2005)	(Wasserstein et al., 2005)	(Wasserstein et al., 2005)

(continued)

Table 7.1. Basic Citation Styles (continued)

Type of citation	First citation in text	Subsequent citations in text	Parenthetical format, first citation in text	Parenthetical format, subsequent citations in text
Groups (readily identified through abbreviation) as authors	National Institute of Mental Health (NIMH, 2003)	NIMH (2003)	(National Institute of Mental Health [NIMH], 2003)	(NIMH, 2003)
Groups (no abbreviation) as authors	University of Pittsburgh (2005)	University of Pittsburgh (2005)	(University of Pittsburgh, 2005)	(University of Pittsburgh, 2005)

Light, M. A., & Light, I. H. (2008). The geographic
    expansion of Mexican immigration in the United
    States and its implications for local law enforce-
    ment. *Law Enforcement Executive Forum
    Journal, 8*, 73–82.

Text Cites:

Among studies, we review M. A. Light and Light
(2008) and I. Light (2006).

7.16 Works With No Identified Author or With an Anonymous Author

When a work has no identified author, cite in text the first
few words of the reference list entry (usually the title) and
the year. Use double quotation marks around the title of
an article, a chapter, or a web page and italicize the title
of a periodical, a book, a brochure, or a report:

on free care ("Study Finds," 2007)

the book *College Bound Seniors* (2008)

Treat references to legal materials like references to works
with no author; that is, in text, cite materials such as court
cases, statutes, and legislation by the first few words of
the reference and the year (see Appendix 8.1 for the format of text citations and references for legal materials).

When a work's author is designated as "Anonymous,"
cite in text the word *Anonymous* followed by a comma and
the date:

(Anonymous, 1998)

In the reference list, an anonymous work is alphabetized
by the word *Anonymous* (see section 7.26).

7.17 Two or More Works Within the Same Parentheses

Order the citations of two or more works within the
same parentheses alphabetically in the same order in

which they appear in the reference list (including citations that would otherwise shorten to *et al.*).

Arrange two or more works by the same authors (in the same order) by year of publication. Place in-press citations last. Give the authors' surnames once; for each subsequent work, give only the date.

> Training materials are available (Department of Veterans Affairs, 2001, 2003)
>
> Past research (Gogel, 1990, 2006, in press)

Identify works by the same author (or by the same two or more authors in the same order) with the same publication date by the suffixes a, b, c, and so forth, after the year; repeat the year. The suffixes are assigned in the reference list, where these kinds of references are ordered alphabetically by title (of the article, chapter, or complete work).

> Several studies (Derryberry & Reed, 2005a, 2005b, in press-a; Rothbart, 2003a, 2003b)

List two or more works by different authors who are cited within the same parentheses in alphabetical order by the first author's surname. Separate the citations with semicolons.

> Several studies (Miller, 1999; Shafranske & Mahoney, 1998)

Exception: You may separate a major citation from other citations within parentheses by inserting a phrase, such as see also, before the first of the remaining citations, which should be in alphabetical order:

> (Minor, 2001; see also Adams, 1999; Storandt, 2007)

7.18 Secondary Sources

Use secondary sources sparingly, for instance, when the original work is out of print, unavailable through usual sources, or not available in English. Give the secondary source in the reference list; in text, name the original work and give a citation for the secondary source. For example, if Allport's work is cited in Nicholson and you did not read Allport's work, list the Nicholson reference in the reference list. In the text, use the following citation:

Allport's diary (as cited in Nicholson, 2003).

7.19 Classical Works

When a date of publication is inapplicable, such as for some very old works, cite the year of the translation you used, preceded by trans., or the year of the version you used, followed by version. When you know the original date of publication, include it in the citation.

(Aristotle, trans. 1931)

James (1890/1983)

Reference list entries are not required for major classical works, such as ancient Greek and Roman works or classical religious works; simply identify in the first citation in the text the version you used. Parts of classical works (e.g., books, chapters, verses, lines, cantos) are numbered systematically across all editions, so use these numbers instead of page numbers when referring to specific parts of your source:

1 Cor. 13:1 (Revised Standard Version)

(Qur'an 5:3–4)

7.20 Citing Specific Parts of a Source

To cite a specific part of a source, indicate the page, chapter, figure, table, or equation at the appropriate point in text. Always give page numbers for quotations (see section 7.03). Note that *page*, but not *chapter*, is abbreviated in such text citations:

(Centers for Disease Control and Prevention, 2005, p. 10)

(Shimamura, 1989, Chapter 3)

For guidance on citing electronic sources that do not provide page numbers, see section 7.05.

7.21 Personal Communications

Personal communications may be private letters, memos, some electronic communications (e.g., e-mail or messages from nonarchived discussion groups or electronic bulletin boards), personal interviews, telephone conversations, and the like. Because they do not provide recoverable data, personal communications are not included in the reference list. Cite personal communications in text only. Give the initials as well as the surname of the communicator, and provide as exact a date as possible:

> T. K. Lutes (personal communication, April 18, 2001)

> (V.-G. Nguyen, personal communication, September 28, 1998)

Use your judgment in citing other electronic forms as personal communications; online networks currently provide a casual forum for communicating, and what you cite should have scholarly relevance.

Some forms of personal communication are recoverable, and these should be referenced as archival materials. See section 8.10 for templates, descriptions, and examples of archival sources in the reference list.

7.22 Citations in Parenthetical Material

In a citation that appears in parenthetical text, use commas, not brackets, to set off the date:

> (see Table 3 of U.S. Department of Labor, 2007, for complete data)

Reference List

The reference list at the end of a journal article provides the information necessary to identify and retrieve each source. Choose references judiciously and include only the sources that you used in the research and preparation of the article. APA journals and other journals using APA Style generally require reference lists, not bibliographies.[1] APA requires that the reference list be double-spaced and that entries have a hanging indent. Because a reference list includes only references that document the article and provide recoverable data, do not include in the list personal communications, such as letters, memoranda, and informal electronic communications. Instead, cite personal communications only in text (see section 7.21 for format).

7.23 Construction of an Accurate and Complete Reference List

Because one purpose of listing references is to enable readers to retrieve and use the sources, reference data must be correct and complete. Each entry usually contains the following elements: author, year of publication, title, and publishing data—all the information necessary for unique identification and library search. The best way to ensure that information is accurate and complete is to check each reference carefully against the original publication. Give special attention to spelling of proper names and of words in foreign languages, including accents or other special marks, and to completeness of journal titles, years, volume and issue numbers, page numbers, and electronic retrieval data. Authors are responsible for all information in their reference lists.

Abbreviations. Acceptable abbreviations in the reference list for parts of books and other publications include the following:

Abbreviation	Book or publication part
ed.	edition
Rev. ed.	Revised edition
2nd ed.	second edition
Ed. (Eds.)	Editor (Editors)

---

[1]Note that a *reference list* cites works that specifically support a particular article. In contrast, a *bibliography* cites works for background or for further reading and may include descriptive notes.

Trans.	Translator(s)
n.d.	no date
p. (pp.)	page (pages)
Vol.	Volume (as in Vol. 4)
Vols.	Volumes (as in Vols. 1–4)
No.	Number
Pt.	Part
Tech. Rep.	Technical Report
Suppl.	Supplement

Arabic numerals. Although some volume numbers of books and journals are given in Roman numerals, APA journals use Arabic numerals (e.g., Vol. 3, not Vol. III) because they use less space and are easier to comprehend than Roman numerals. A Roman numeral that is part of a title should remain Roman (e.g., *Attention and Performance XIII*).

7.24 Consistency

Consistency in reference style is important, especially in light of evolving technologies in database indexing, such as automatic indexing by database crawlers. These computer programs use algorithms to capture data from primary articles as well as from the article reference list. If reference elements are out of order or incomplete, the algorithm may not recognize them, lowering the likelihood that the reference will be captured for indexing. With this in mind, follow the general formats for placement of data and use the electronic reference guidelines detailed in this chapter to decide which data are necessary to allow readers to access the sources you used.

7.25 Using the Archival Copy or Version of Record

When using information and data retrieved online, check to see whether you are citing the appropriate version of your reference source. In-progress and final versions of the same work might coexist on the Internet, which can present challenges in determining which version is most current and most authoritative. In most cases, it is best to cite the archival version or version of record, which has been peer-reviewed and may provide additional links to online supplemental material. If the most current version available was an advance release version at the time that you originally cited it, recheck the source and update its publication status as close as possible to the publication date of your work.

7.26 Order of References in the Reference List

The principles for arranging entries in a reference list are described next. You may also find it helpful to look at reference lists in journals that are published in APA Style.

Alphabetizing names. Arrange entries in alphabetical order by the surname of the first author followed by initials of the author's given name, and use the following rules for special cases:

- Alphabetize by the author's surname. This surname/given name formula is commonly used in Western countries but is less commonly used in many Eastern countries. If you are uncertain about the proper format for a name, check with the author for the preferred form or consult the author's previous publication for the commonly used form (e.g., Chen Zhe may publish under Zhe Chen in the United States).
- Alphabetize letter by letter. When alphabetizing surnames, remember that "nothing precedes something": Brown, J. R., precedes Browning, A. R., even though *i* precedes *j* in the alphabet.

Singh, Y., precedes Singh Siddhu, N.

López, M. E., precedes López de Molina, G.

Ibn Abdulaziz, T., precedes Ibn Nidal, A. K. M.

Girard, J.-B., precedes Girard-Perregaux, A. S.

> Villafuerte, S. A., precedes Villa-Lobos, J.
>
> Benjamin, A. S., precedes ben Yaakov, D.

■ Alphabetize the prefixes M', Mc, and Mac literally, not as if they were all spelled *Mac*. Disregard the apostrophe: MacArthur precedes McAllister, and MacNeil precedes M'Carthy.

■ Alphabetize entries with numerals chronologically (e.g., Macomber, J., II, precedes Macomber, J., III).

Order of several works by the same first author. When ordering several works by the same first author, give the author's name in the first and all subsequent references, and use the following rules to arrange the entries:

■ One-author entries by the same author are arranged by year of publication, the earliest first:

> Upenieks, V. (2003).
>
> Upenieks, V. (2005).

■ One-author entries precede multiple-author entries beginning with the same surname (even if the multiple-author work was published earlier):

> Alleyne, R. L. (2001).
>
> Alleyne, R. L., & Evans, A. J. (1999).

■ References with the same first author and different second or third authors are arranged alphabetically by the surname of the second author or, if the second author is the same, the surname of the third author, and so on:

> Boockvar, K. S., & Burack, O. R. (2007).
>
> Boockvar, K. S., Carlson LaCorte, H., Giambanco, V., Friedman, B., & Siu, A. (2006).
>
> Hayward, D., Firsching, A., & Brown, J. (1999).
>
> Hayward, D., Firsching, A., & Smigel, J. (1999).

- References with the same authors in the same order are arranged by year of publication, the earliest first:

> Cabading, J. R., & Wright, K. (2000).
>
> Cabading, J. R., & Wright, K. (2001).

- References by the same author (or by the same two or more authors in the same order) with the same publication date are arranged alphabetically by title (excluding *A* or *The*).

Exception: If the references with the same authors published in the same year are identified as articles in a series (e.g., Part 1 and Part 2), order the references in the series order, not alphabetically by title.

Place lowercase letters—*a, b, c,* and so on—immediately after the year, within the parentheses:

> Baheti, J. R. (2001a). Control . . .
>
> Baheti, J. R. (2001b). Roles of . . .

Order of several works by different first authors with the same surname. Arrange works by different authors with the same surname alphabetically by first initial:

> Mathur, A. L., & Wallston, J. (1999).
>
> Mathur, S. E., & Ahlers, R. J. (1998).

Note: Include initials with the surname of the first author in text citations (see section 7.15).

Order of works with group authors or with no authors. Occasionally, a work will have as its author an agency, association, or institution, or it will have no author at all.

Alphabetize group authors, such as associations or government agencies, by the first significant word of the name. Full official names should be used (e.g., American Psychological Association, not APA). A parent body precedes a subdivision (e.g., University of Michigan, Department of Psychology).

If, and only if, the work is signed "Anonymous," begin the entry with the word *Anonymous* spelled out, and alphabetize the entry as if Anonymous were a true name.

If there is no author, move the title to the author position, and alphabetize the entry by the first significant word of the title.

Treat legal references like references with no author; that is, alphabetize legal references by the first significant item in the entry (word or abbreviation). See Appendix 8.1 for the format of references for legal materials and ways to cite them in the text.

7.27 References Included in a Meta-Analysis

If the number of articles contributing studies to the meta-analysis is relatively small (e.g., about 50 or fewer), they should appear in the reference list with an asterisk included to identify them. If the number of articles in the meta-analysis exceeds 50, then the references to the articles should be placed in a list and submitted as an online supplemental archive. In this second case, if an article is mentioned in the text and is included in the meta-analysis, it should be cited both in the reference list and in the supplemental materials.

Add the following statement before the first reference entry: *References marked with an asterisk indicate studies included in the meta-analysis.* The in-text citations to studies selected for meta-analysis are not preceded by asterisks.

> Bandura, A. J. (1977). *Social learning theory.* Englewood Cliffs, NJ: Prentice Hall.
>
> *Bretschneider, J. G., & McCoy, N. L. (1968). Sexual interest and behavior in healthy 80- to 102-year-olds. *Archives of Sexual Behavior, 14,* 343–350.

Reference Components

In general, a reference should contain the author name, date of publication, title of the work, and publication data. The following sections (7.28–7.32) describe these components. Detailed notes on style accompany the description of each element, and example numbers given in parentheses correspond to examples given in Chapter 8.

7.28 Author and Editor Information

Authors.

- Invert all authors' names; give surnames and initials for up to and including seven authors (e.g., Author, A. A., Author, B. B., & Author, C. C.). When authors number eight or more, include the first six authors' names, then insert three ellipsis points, and add the last author's name (see Chapter 8, Example 2). In text, follow the citation guidelines in section 7.13.

- If the reference list includes different authors with the same surname and first initial, the authors' full first names may be given in brackets:

> Janet, P. [Paul]. (1876). La notion de la personnalité [The notion of personality]. *Revue Scientifique, 10,* 574–575.

> Janet, P. [Pierre]. (1906). The pathogenesis of some impulsions. *Journal of Abnormal Psychology, 1,* 1–17.

In text:

> (Paul Janet, 1876)

> (Pierre Janet, 1906)

- If an author's first name is hyphenated, retain the hyphen and include a period after each initial (Lamour, J.-B., for Jean-Baptiste Lamour).

- Use commas to separate authors, to separate surnames and initials, and to separate initials and suffixes (e.g., Jr. and III; see Chapter 8, Example 24); with two to seven authors, use an ampersand (&) before the last author.

- Spell out the full name of a group author (e.g., Royal Institute of Technology; National Institute of Mental Health; see Chapter 8, Examples 31, 32, 35, 68). In a reference to a work with a group author (e.g., study group, government agency, association, corporation), a period follows the author element.
- If authors are listed with the word *with*, include them in the reference in parentheses: Bulatao, E. (with Winford, C. A.). The text citation, however, refers to the primary author only.
- In a reference to a work with no author, move the title to the author position, before the date of publication (see Chapter 8, Examples 9, 30, 71). A period follows the title.

Editors.

- In a reference to an edited book, place the editors' names in the author position, and enclose the abbreviation Ed. or Eds. in parentheses after the last editor's name. The period follows the parenthetical abbreviation (Eds.).
- In a reference to a chapter in an edited book, invert the chapter authors' names as noted above but do not invert book editors' names.
- The name of the book editor should be preceded by the word *In*. Provide initials and surnames for all editors (for substantial reference works with a large editorial board, naming the lead editor followed by et al. is acceptable).

> Author, A. A. (2008). Title of chapter. In E. E. Editor (Ed.), *Title of book* (pp. xx–xx). Location: Publisher.

- For a book with no editor, simply include the word In before the book title.

7.29 Publication Date

- Give in parentheses the year the work was published (for unpublished or informally published works, give the year the work was produced).

- For magazines, newsletters, and newspapers, give the year and the exact date of the publication (month or month and day), separated by a comma and enclosed in parentheses (see Chapter 8, Examples 7–11). If the date is given as a season, give the year and the season, separated by a comma and enclosed in parentheses.
- For papers and posters presented at meetings, give the year and month of the meeting, separated by a comma and enclosed in parentheses.
- Write in press in parentheses for articles that have been accepted for publication but that have not yet been published (see Chapter 8, Example 6). Do not give a date until the article has actually been published. (To reference a paper that is still in progress, under review, or being revised, see Chapter 8, Example 59.)
- If no date is available, write n.d. in parentheses.
- For several volumes in a multivolume work or several letters from the same collection, express the date as a range of years from earliest to latest (see Chapter 8, Examples 23 and 65).
- For archival sources, indicate an estimated date that is reasonably certain but not stated on the document by using ca. (circa) and enclose the information in square brackets (see Chapter 8, Example 67).
- Finish the element with a period after the closing parenthesis.

7.30 Title

Article or chapter title. Capitalize only the first word of the title and of the subtitle, if any, and any proper nouns; do not italicize the title or place quotation marks around it. Finish the element with a period.

> Mental and nervous diseases in the Russo-Japanese war: A historical analysis.

Periodical title: Journals, newsletters, magazines. Give the periodical title in full, in uppercase and lowercase letters. Italicize the name of the periodical.

> *Social Science Quarterly*

Nonperiodical title: Books and reports.

- Capitalize only the first word of the title and of the subtitle, if any, and any proper nouns; italicize the title.
- Enclose additional information given on the publication for its identification and retrieval (e.g., edition, report number, volume number) in parentheses immediately after the title. Do not use a period between the title and the parenthetical information; do not italicize the parenthetical information.

> *Development of entry-level tests to select FBI special agents* (Publication No. FR-PRD-94–06).

- If a volume is part of a larger, separately titled series or collection, treat the series and volume titles as a two-part title (see Chapter 8, Example 24).
- Finish the element with a period.

Nonroutine information in titles. If nonroutine information is important for identification and retrieval, provide it in brackets immediately after the title and any parenthetical information. Capitalize the first letter of the notation. Brackets indicate a description of form, not a title. Here are some of the more common notations that help identify works:

Notation

[Letter to the editor]

[Special issue]

[Special section]

[Monograph]

[Abstract]

[Audio podcast]

[Data file]

[Brochure]

[Motion picture]

[Lecture notes]

[CD]

[Computer software]

[Video webcast]

[Supplemental material]

7.31 Publication Information

Periodicals: Journals, newsletters, magazines.

- Give the volume number after the periodical title; italicize it. Do not use Vol. before the number.

- Include the journal issue number (if available) along with the volume number if the journal is paginated separately by issue (see Chapter 8, Examples 3, 7, 8). Give the issue number in parentheses immediately after the volume number; do not italicize it. Give inclusive page numbers on which the cited material appears.

- Finish the element with a period.

    Social Science Quarterly, 84, 508–525.

- Periodical publisher names and locations are generally not included in references, in accordance with long practice.

Nonperiodicals: Books and reports.

- Give the location (city and state or, if outside of the United States, city and country) where the publisher is located as noted on the title page for books; reports; brochures; and other separate, nonperiodical publications.

- If the publisher is a university and the name of the state or province is included in the name of the university, do not repeat the name in the publisher location.

- The names of U.S. states and territories are abbreviated in the reference list and in the Method section (suppliers' locations); use the official two-letter U.S.

Postal Service abbreviations. To cite locations outside the United States, spell out the city and the country names. However, if you are publishing outside the United States or for an international readership, check your institution's or publisher's specific style guidelines for writing out or abbreviating state, province, territory, and country names.

■ Use a colon after the location.

■ Give the name of the publisher in as brief a form as is intelligible. Write out the names of associations, corporations, and university presses, but omit superfluous terms, such as *Publishers*, *Co.*, and *Inc.*, which are not required to identify the publisher. Retain the words *Books* and *Press*.

■ If two or more publisher locations are given in the book, give the location listed first or, if specified, the location of the publisher's home office.

■ When the author is also the publisher, use *Author* to indicate the publisher.

■ Finish the element with a period.

New York, NY: McGraw-Hill.

Washington, DC: Author.

Newbury Park, CA: Sage.

Pretoria, South Africa: Unisa.

7.32 Electronic Sources and Locator Information

Since this manual was last updated, electronic journal publishing has gone from being the exception to the rule. Publishing in the online environment has greatly increased the efficiency of publication processes and has contributed to a more vibrant and timely sharing of research results. However, the electronic dissemination of information has also led to a number of new publishing models. Unedited articles can now be disseminated on the Internet in advance of publication. Links to supplementary material such as long data sets and videos can be embedded in electronic articles and made accessible with a simple click. Corrections that were formerly noted in a subsequent journal issue can now be made with no fanfare as a simple update to online files. All of these circumstances have called for new ways of tracking digital information.

In this new environment, some former models for referencing material no longer apply. It is not always clear how to distinguish the advance online version of an article from the final published version or how to determine which is the "version of record" (see section 7.25). Moreover, readers may be consulting the electronic version with supplemental material or the print version of the same article without supplemental material. In the ephemeral world of the web, article links are not always robust.

In general, we recommend that you include the same elements, in the same order, as you would for a reference to a fixed-media source and add as much electronic retrieval information as needed for others to locate the sources you cited. We discuss next some key elements of the electronic retrieval process, beginning with some general information about uniform resource locators (URLs) and digital object identifiers (DOIs) and ending with formatting guidance for citing publication data from electronic sources.

Understanding a URL. The URL is used to map digital information on the Internet. The components of a URL are as follows:

Protocol indicates what method a web browser (or other type of Internet software) should use to exchange data with the file server on which the desired document resides. The protocols recognized by most browsers are hypertext transfer protocol (HTTP), hypertext transfer protocol secure (HTTPS), and file transfer protocol (FTP). In a URL, the protocol is followed by a colon and two forward slashes (e.g., http://).

Host or *domain name* identifies the server on which the files reside. On the web, it is often the address for an organization's home page (e.g., http://www.apa.org is the address for APA's home page). Although many domain names start with "www," not all do (e.g., http://journals.apa.org is the home page for APA's electronic journals, and http://members.apa.org is the entry page to the members-only portion of the APA site). The domain name is not case sensitive; for consistency and ease of reading, always type it in lowercase letters.

The domain name extension (in the preceding example, ".org") can help you determine the appropriateness of the source for your purpose. Different extensions are used depending on what entity hosts the site. For example, the extensions ".edu" and ".org" are for educational institutions and nonprofit organizations, respectively; ".gov" and ".mil" are used for government and military sites, respectively; and ".com" and ".biz" are used for commercial sites. Domain name extensions may also include a country code (e.g., ".ca" for Canada or ".nz" for New Zealand). The rest of the address indicates the directory path leading to the desired document.

All content on the Internet is prone to being moved, restructured, or deleted, resulting in broken hyperlinks and nonworking URLs in the reference list. In an attempt to resolve this problem, scholarly publishers have begun assigning a DOI to journal articles and other documents.

The DOI system. Developed by a group of international publishers, the DOI System provides a means of persistent identification for managing information on digital networks (see http://www.doi.org/). The DOI System is implemented through registration agencies such as CrossRef, which provides citation-linking services for the scientific publishing sector. According to their mission statement, CrossRef is dedicated "to enable easy identification and use of trustworthy electronic content by promoting the cooperative development and application of a sustainable infrastructure" (http://www.crossref.org/).

CrossRef's participants have developed a system that provides two critical functions. First, they assign each article a "unique identifier and underlying routing system" that functions as a clearinghouse to direct readers to content, regardless of where the content resides (Kasdorf, 2003, p. 646). Second, they collaborate to use the DOI as an underlying linking mechanism "embedded" in the reference lists of electronic articles that allows click-through access to each reference. CrossRef currently has more than 2,600 participating publishers and scholarly societies.

The DOI as article identifier. A DOI is a unique alphanumeric string assigned by a registration agency (the International DOI Foundation) to identify content and provide a persistent link to its location on the Internet.

The publisher assigns a DOI when your article is published and made available electronically. All DOI numbers begin with a *10* and contain a prefix and a suffix separated by a slash. The prefix is a unique number of four or more digits assigned to organizations; the suffix is assigned by the publisher and was designed to be flexible with publisher identification standards. We recommend that when DOIs are available, you include them for both print and electronic sources.

The DOI is typically located on the first page of the electronic journal article, near the copyright notice (see

Figure 7.2. Location of Digital Object Identifier (DOI) in Journal Article

Journal of Experimental Psychology:
Learning, Memory, and Cognition
2008, Vol. 34, No. 3, 439–459

Copyright 2008 by the American Psychological Association
0278-7393/08/$12.00 DOI: 10.1037/0278-7393.34.3.439

How to Say No: Single- and Dual-Process Theories of Short-Term
Recognition Tested on Negative Probes

Klaus Oberauer
University of Bristol

Three experiments with short-term recognition tasks are reported. In Experiments 1 and 2, participants decided whether a probe matched a list item specified by its spatial location. Items presented at a study

Figure 7.3. Location of Digital Object Identifier for Article on Database Landing Page

Full Record Display

Unique Identifier
> 2008-08834-010

Title
> A taxonomy of behavior change techniques used in interventions.

Publication Year
> 2008

Language
> English

Author
> <u>Abraham, Charles</u> ; <u>Michie, Susan</u>

Email
> Abraham, Charles: s.c.s.abraham@sussex.ac.uk

Correspondence Address
> Charles Abraham, Department of Psychology, University of Sussex, Falmer, Brighton, England, BN1 9QG, s.c.s.abraham@sussex.ac.uk

Affiliation

Abraham, Charles	Department of Psychology, University of Sussex, Brighton, England
Michie, Susan	Department of Psychology, University College London, London, England

Source
> Health Psychology. Vol 27(3), May 2008, 379-387.

ISSN
> 0278-6133 (Print); 1930-7810 (Electronic)

Publisher
> American Psychological Association: US

Other Publishers
> Lawrence Erlbaum Associates, US

Format Availability
> Electronic; Print

Format Covered
> Electronic

Publication Type
> Journal; Peer Reviewed Journal

Document Type
> Journal Article

Digital Object Identifier
> <u>10.1037/0278-6133.27.3.379</u>

Keywords
> behavior change; intervention; content; techniques; taxonomy; CONSORT

Index Terms
> <u>*Behavior Change</u>; <u>*Health Promotion</u>; <u>*Intervention</u>; <u>*Taxonomies</u>

Classification Codes
> <u>3300 Health & Mental Health Treatment & Prevention</u>

Population Group
> Human

Methodology
> 0400 Empirical Study; 1800 Quantitative Study

Auxiliary Materials
> Other (Internet Available)

Release Date
> 20080714

Figure 7.2). The DOI can also be found on the database landing page for the article (see Figure 7.3).

> ***The linking function of DOIs.*** The DOIs in the reference list function as links to the content you are referencing. The DOI may be hidden under a button labeled *Article,*

Figure 7.4. Example of Reference in Electronic Document With Digital Object Identifier Hidden Behind a Button

```
<ref>Hedges, L. V., & Vevea, J. L. (1998). Fixed- and random-
    effects models in meta-analysis. Psychological Methods, 3,
    486<en>504.  PsycINFO   Article
```

CrossRef, PubMed, or another full-text vendor name (see Figure 7.4). Readers can then click on the button to view the actual article or to view an abstract and an opportunity to purchase a copy of the item. If the link is not live or if the DOI is referenced in a print publication, the reader can simply enter the DOI into the DOI *resolver* search field provided by the registration agency CrossRef.org and be directed to the article or a link to purchase it (see Figure 7.5). Locating the article online with the DOI will give you electronic access to any on-

Figure 7.5. Digital Object Identifier Resolver

Source: crossref.org

line supplemental archives associated with the article (see section 6.04 regarding supplemental materials).

7.33 Providing Publication Data for Electronic Sources

- For electronic versions based on a print source (as in PDF), give inclusive page numbers for the article cited. Use pp. before the page numbers in references to newspapers. See Chapter 8, Examples 1–3.

- Provide the DOI, if one has been assigned to the content. Publishers who follow best practices publish the DOI prominently on the first page of an article. Because the DOI string can be long, it is safest to copy and paste whenever possible. Provide the alphanumeric string for the DOI exactly as published in the article. This is not a style issue but a retrieval issue.

- Use this format for the DOI in references: doi:xxxxxxx

- When a DOI is used, no further retrieval information is needed to identify or locate the content.

- If no DOI has been assigned to the content, provide the home page URL of the journal or of the book or report publisher. If you are accessing the article from a private database, you may need to do a quick web search to locate this URL. Transcribe the URL correctly by copying it directly from the address window in your browser and pasting it into your working document (make sure the automatic hyphenation feature of your word processor is turned off).

- Do not insert a hyphen if you need to break a URL across lines; instead, break the URL before most punctuation (an exception would be http://). Do not add a period after the URL, to prevent the impression that the period is part of the URL. This is not a style issue but a retrieval issue.

- Test URLs in your references at each stage prior to the submission and/or publication of your work. If the document you are citing has moved, update the URL so that it points to the correct location. If the content is no longer available, substitute another source (i.e., the final version if you originally cited a draft) or drop it from the paper altogether.

- In general, it is not necessary to include database information. Journal coverage in a particular database may change over time; also, if using an aggregator such as EBSCO, OVID, or ProQuest (each of which contain many discipline-specific databases, such as PsycINFO), it may be unclear exactly which database provided the full text of an article.

- Some archival documents (e.g., discontinued journals, monographs, dissertations, or papers not formally published) can only be found in electronic databases such as ERIC or JSTOR. When the document is not easily located through its primary publishing channels, give the home or entry page URL for the online archive.

- Do not include retrieval dates unless the source material may change over time (e.g., wikis).

- As with references to material in print or other fixed media, it is preferable to cite the final version (i.e., archival copy or version of record; see section 7.25).

8

Reference Examples

This chapter contains examples of references in APA Style. The examples are grouped into categories and, in most cases, references to electronic or downloadable versions of each source type are integrated with references to print or fixed media versions.

The most common kinds of references are illustrated herein. Occasionally, however, you may need to cite a source for which this chapter does not provide specific guidance. In such a case, choose the example that is most like your source and follow that format. Provide more information rather than less, keeping in mind that most entries contain the following elements: author, year of publication, title, and publishing or retrieval data—all the information necessary for unique identification and library search. Additional reference examples may be found on the APA Style website (www.apastyle.org).

Following is an index to the reference examples that lists types of work referenced and variations of each reference element. The numbers after each index entry refer to the numbered reference examples. Appendix 8.1 at the end of this chapter includes templates and example references to legal materials.

Types and Variations
Periodicals

Books, Reference Books, and Book Chapters

Technical and Research Reports

Meetings and Symposia

Doctoral Dissertations and Master's Theses

Reviews and Peer Commentary

Audiovisual Media

Data Sets, Software, Measurement Instruments, and Apparatus

Unpublished and Informally Published Works

Archival Documents and Collections

Internet Message Boards, Electronic Mailing Lists, and Other Online Communities

Author Variations

Title Variations

Publication Information Variations

Examples by Type

8.01 Periodicals

Periodicals include items published on a regular basis such as journals, magazines, newspapers, and newsletters.

General reference form:

> Author, A. A., Author, B. B., & Author, C. C. (year). Title of article. *Title of Periodical, xx*, pp–pp. doi:xx.xxxxxxxxxx

- Include the digital object identifier (DOI) in the reference if one is assigned (see section 7.32)
- If no DOI is assigned to the content and you retrieved it online, include the home page URL for the journal, newsletter, or magazine in the reference. Use this format: Retrieved from http://xxxxxxxx
- If each issue of a journal begins on page 1, give the issue number in parentheses immediately after the volume number.
- If you are citing an advance release version of the article, insert Advance online publication before the retrieval statement.
- Some journals offer supplemental material that is available only online. To reference this supplemental material, or any other nonroutine information that is important for identification and retrieval, include a description of the content in brackets following the title: [Letter to the editor], [Map], [Audio podcast].

1. Journal article with DOI

Herbst-Damm, K. L., & Kulik, J. A. (2005). Volunteer support, marital status, and the survival times of terminally ill patients. *Health Psychology, 24*, 225–229. doi:10.1037/0278-6133.24.2.225

2. Journal article with DOI, more than seven authors

Gilbert, D. G., McClernon, J. F., Rabinovich, N. E., Sugai, C., Plath, L. C., Asgaard, G, . . . Botros, N. (2004). Effects of quitting smoking on EEG activation and attention last for more than 31 days and are more severe with stress, dependence, DRD2 A1 allele, and depressive traits. *Nicotine and Tobacco Research, 6*, 249–267. doi:10.1080/14622200410001676305

■ Use the following in-text citation: (Gilbert et al., 2004).
■ When a reference has up to seven authors, spell out all authors' names in the reference list.

3. Journal article without DOI (when DOI is not available)

Sillick, T. J., & Schutte, N. S. (2006). Emotional intelligence and self-esteem mediate between perceived early parental love and adult happiness. *E-Journal of Applied Psychology, 2*(2), 38–48. Retrieved from http://ojs.lib.swin.edu.au/index.php/ejap

Light, M. A., & Light, I. H. (2008). The geographic expansion of Mexican immigration in the United States and its implications for local law enforcement. *Law Enforcement Executive Forum Journal, 8*(1), 73–82.

■ Include the issue number if the journal is paginated by issue.
■ If there is no DOI assigned and the reference was retrieved online, give the URL of the journal home page.
■ No retrieval date is needed.

4. Journal article without DOI, title translated into English, print version

Guimard, P., & Florin, A. (2007). Les évaluations des enseignants en grande section de maternelle sont-elles prédictives des difficultés de lecture au cours préparatoire? [Are teacher ratings in kindergarten predictive of reading difficulties in first grade?]. *Approche Neuropsychologique des Apprentissages chez l'Enfant, 19,* 5–17.

- If the original version of a non-English article is used as the source, cite the original version. Give the original title and, in brackets, the English translation.
- If the English translation of a non-English article is used as the source, cite the English translation. Give the English title without brackets.

5. Journal article with DOI, advance online publication

Von Ledebur, S. C. (2007). Optimizing knowledge transfer by new employees in companies. *Knowledge Management Research & Practice.* Advance online publication. doi:10.1057 /palgrave.kmrp.8500141

- This journal publishes four print issues per year but also offers individual articles online as soon as they are finalized. The content is assigned a DOI before it is assigned a volume, issue, or page numbers.
- If there is no DOI assigned and you retrieved the article electronically, give the URL of the journal home page.
- Definitions of *advance online publication* vary among journal publishers. Generally, the term refers to peer-reviewed work, but the content may not be copyedited or formatted for final production.
- Update your references close to the publication date of your work, and refer to final versions of your sources, if possible.

6. In-press article posted in a preprint archive

> Briscoe, R. (in press). Egocentric spatial representation in action and perception. *Philosophy and Phenomenological Research*. Retrieved from http://cogprints.org/5780/1/ECSRAP.F07.pdf

- The exact URL is used because the article is informally published and not yet indexed on a journal website. Journal publishers that do not offer advance online publication may allow authors to post a version of their article online ahead of print in an outside repository, also called a *preprint archive*.
- Update your references close to the publication date of your work and refer to the final version of a work, if possible.

7. Magazine article

> Chamberlin, J., Novotney, A., Packard, E., & Price, M. (2008, May). Enhancing worker well-being: Occupational health psychologists convene to share their research on work, stress, and health. *Monitor on Psychology, 39*(5), 26–29.

8. Online magazine article

> Clay, R. (2008, June). Science vs. ideology: Psychologists fight back about the misuse of research. *Monitor on Psychology, 39*(6). Retrieved from http://www.apa.org/monitor/

9. Newsletter article, no author

> Six sites meet for comprehensive anti-gang initiative conference. (2006, November/December). *OJJDP News @ a Glance*. Retrieved from http://www.ncjrs.gov/html/ojjdp/news_at_glance/216684/topstory.html

- The exact URL is helpful here because specific newsletter articles are difficult to locate from the government agency home page.

- Alphabetize works with no author by the first significant word in the title (in this case, "Six").
- In text, use a short title (or the full title if it is short) enclosed in quotation marks for the parenthetical citation: ("Six Sites Meet," 2006).

10. Newspaper article

> Schwartz, J. (1993, September 30). Obesity affects economic, social status. *The Washington Post*, pp. A1, A4.

- Precede page numbers for newspaper articles with p. or pp.
- If an article appears on discontinuous pages, give all page numbers, and separate the numbers with a comma (e.g., pp. B1, B3, B5–B7).

11. Online newspaper article

> Brody, J. E. (2007, December 11). Mental reserves keep brain agile. *The New York Times*. Retrieved from http://www.nytimes.com

- Give the URL of the home page when the online version of the article is available by search to avoid non-working URLs.

12. Special issue or section in a journal

> Haney, C., & Wiener, R. L. (Eds.). (2004). Capital punishment in the United States [Special issue]. *Psychology, Public Policy, and Law, 10*(4).

> Greenfield, P., & Yan, Z. (Eds.). (2006). Children, adolescents, and the Internet [Special section]. *Developmental Psychology, 42*, 391–394. doi: 10.1037/0012-1649.42.3.391

- To cite an entire issue or special section of a journal, give the editors of the issue and the title of the issue.
- If the issue has no editors, move the issue title to the author position, before the year of publication, and end the title with a period. Alphabetize the reference entry

by the first significant word in the title. In text, use a shortened title enclosed in quotation marks for the parenthetical citation: ("Capital Punishment," 2004).

■ Provide the page range for special sections.

■ To reference an article within a special issue, simply follow the format shown in Examples 1–4.

13. Monograph as part of journal issue

Ganster, D. C., Schaubroeck, J., Sime, W. E., & Mayes, B. T. (1991). The nomological validity of the Type A personality among employed adults [Monograph]. *Journal of Applied Psychology, 76,* 143–168. doi:10.1037/0021-9010.76.1.143

■ For a monograph with an issue (or whole) number, include the issue number in parentheses followed by the serial number, for example, *58*(1, Serial No. 231).

■ For a monograph bound separately as a supplement to a journal, give the issue number and supplement or part number in parentheses after the volume number, for example, *80*(3, Pt. 2).

14. Editorial without signature

Editorial: "What is a disaster" and why does this question matter? [Editorial]. (2006). *Journal of Contingencies and Crisis Management, 14,* 1–2.

15. Online-only supplemental material in a periodical

Marshall-Pescini, S., & Whiten, A. (2008). Social learning of nut-cracking behavior in East African sanctuary-living chimpanzees (*Pan troglodytes schweinfurthii*) [Supplemental material]. *Journal of Comparative Psychology, 122,* 186–194. doi:10.1037/0735-7036.122.2.186.supp

■ The description of supplemental material or other non-routine information (e.g., a letter to the editor, podcast, or map) is included in brackets to help the reader identify and retrieve the material.

- For a letter to the editor or other special material in a periodical, provide a description of the material in brackets following the title.
- If no author is indicated, move the title and bracketed description to the author position.
- In text, use the following parenthetical citation (Marshall-Pescini & Whiten, 2008).

16. Abstract as original source

Woolf, N. J., Young, S. L., Fanselow, M. S., & Butcher, L. L. (1991). MAP-2 expression in cholinoceptive pyramidal cells of rodent cortex and hippocampus is altered by Pavlovian conditioning [Abstract]. *Society for Neuroscience Abstracts, 17,* 480.

Lassen, S. R., Steele, M. M., & Sailor, W. (2006). The relationship of school-wide positive behavior support to academic achievement in an urban middle school. *Psychology in the Schools, 43,* 701–712. Abstract retrieved from http://www.interscience.wiley.com

- Although it is preferable to cite the full text of an article, abstracts can be used as sources and included in the reference list.

17. Abstract as secondary source

Hare, L. R., & O'Neill, K. (2000). Effectiveness and efficiency in small academic peer groups. *Small Group Research, 31,* 24–53. Abstract retrieved from Sociological Abstracts database. (Accession No. 200010185)

- Although it is preferable to cite the full text of an article, abstracts can be used as sources and included in the reference list.
- Database names and abstract identifier (if applicable) may be given for material of limited circulation.

8.02 Books, Reference Books, and Book Chapters

This category includes books and reference books such as encyclopedias, dictionaries, and discipline-specific reference books (e.g., *Diagnostic and Statistical Manual of Mental Disorders*). It also includes books that are published in electronic form only, reference works and public domain books available online, and out-of-print books that may be available only in online repositories. When DOIs are assigned, use them as noted in the examples that follow.

For an entire book, use the following reference formats:

> Author, A. A. (1967). *Title of work.* Location: Publisher.
>
> Author, A. A. (1997). *Title of work.* Retrieved from http://www.xxxxxxx
>
> Author, A. A. (2006). *Title of work.* doi:xxxxx
>
> Editor, A. A. (Ed.). (1986). *Title of work.* Location: Publisher.

For a chapter in a book or entry in a reference book, use the following formats:

> Author, A. A., & Author, B. B. (1995). Title of chapter or entry. In A. Editor, B. Editor, & C. Editor (Eds.), *Title of book* (pp. xxx–xxx). Location: Publisher.
>
> Author, A. A., & Author, B. B. (1993). Title of chapter or entry. In A. Editor & B. Editor (Eds.), *Title of book* (pp. xxx–xxx). Retrieved from http://www.xxxxxxx
>
> Author, A. A., & Author, B. B. (1995). Title of chapter or entry. In A. Editor, B. Editor, & C. Editor (Eds.), *Title of book* (pp. xxx–xxx). doi:xxxxxxxx

■ If there are no page numbers, the chapter or entry title is sufficient.

For an entry in a reference work with no byline, use the following formats:

> Title of entry. (1998). In A. Editor (Ed.), *Title of reference work* (xx ed., Vol. xx, pp. xxx–xxx). Location: Publisher.

> Title of entry. (1998). In *Title of reference work* (xx ed., Vol. xx). Retrieved from http://www.xxxxxxxxx

- When the author and publisher are the same, use the word *Author* as the name of the publisher.
- Alphabetize books with no author or editor by the first significant word in the title. In the text citation, use a few words of the title, or the whole title if it is short, in place of an author name.
- Place information about editions, volume numbers, and page numbers (such as revised edition, volume number, or chapter page range) in parentheses following the title, with the period after the parentheses: (Rev. ed.) or (Vol. xx, pp. xxx–xxx).
- For major reference works with a large editorial board, you may list the name of the lead editor, followed by *et al.*
- For books or chapters available only online, the electronic retrieval statement takes the place of publisher location and name (see Examples 19–22, 24).

18. Entire book, print version

> Shotton, M. A. (1989). *Computer addiction? A study of computer dependency.* London, England: Taylor & Francis.

19. Electronic version of print book

> Shotton, M. A. (1989). *Computer addiction? A study of computer dependency* [DX Reader version]. Retrieved from http://www.ebookstore.tandf.co.uk/html/index.asp

> Schiraldi, G. R. (2001). *The post-traumatic stress disorder sourcebook: A guide to healing, recov-*

ery, and growth [Adobe Digital Editions version].
doi:10.1036/0071393722

20. Electronic-only book

O'Keefe, E. (n.d.). *Egoism & the crisis in Western values.* Retrieved from http://www.onlineoriginals.com/showitem.asp?itemID=135

21. Electronic version of republished book

Freud, S. (1953). The method of interpreting dreams: An analysis of a specimen dream. In J. Strachey (Ed. & Trans.), *The standard edition of the complete psychological works of Sigmund Freud* (Vol. 4, pp. 96–121). Retrieved from http://books.google.com/books (Original work published 1900)

■ In text, use the following citation: (Freud, 1900/1953).

22. Limited-circulation book or monograph, from electronic database

Thomas, N. (Ed.). (2002). *Perspectives on the community college: A journey of discovery* [Monograph]. Retrieved from http://eric.ed.gov/

■ Database information may be given for items of limited circulation.

23. Several volumes in a multivolume work

Koch, S. (Ed.). (1959–1963). *Psychology: A study of science* (Vols. 1–6). New York, NY: McGraw-Hill.

■ In text, use the following parenthetical citation: (Koch, 1959–1963).

24. Electronic version of book chapter in a volume in a series

Strong, E. K., Jr., & Uhrbrock, R. S. (1923). Bibliography on job analysis. In L. Outhwaite

(Series Ed.), *Personnel Research Series: Vol. 1.
Job analysis and the curriculum* (pp. 140–146).
doi:10.1037/10762-000

- If the content has been assigned a DOI, give the
DOI in the reference. No URL or database name is
needed.
- In regularly published series with subtitles that change
regularly, the series title is uppercase and the subtitle is
lowercase, as in a book title.

25. Book chapter, print version

Haybron, D. M. (2008). Philosophy and the science
of subjective well-being. In M. Eid & R. J. Larsen
(Eds.), *The science of subjective well-being* (pp.
17–43). New York, NY: Guilford Press.

26. Book chapter, English translation, reprinted from another source

Piaget, J. (1988). Extracts from Piaget's theory (G.
Gellerier & J. Langer, Trans.). In K. Richardson &
S. Sheldon (Eds.), *Cognitive development to adolescence: A reader* (pp. 3–18). Hillsdale, NJ:
Erlbaum. (Reprinted from *Manual of child psychology*, pp. 703–732, by P. H. Mussen, Ed.,
1970, New York, NY: Wiley)

- If the English translation of a non-English work is used
as the source, cite the English translation. Give the
English title without brackets, followed by the translator's name in parentheses.
- In text, use the following parenthetical citation:
(Piaget, 1970/1988).

27. Reference book

VandenBos, G. R. (Ed.). (2007). *APA dictionary of
psychology*. Washington, DC: American Psychological Association.

28. Non-English reference book, title translated into English

> Real Academia Española. (2001). *Diccionario de la lengua española* [Dictionary of the Spanish language] (22nd ed.). Madrid, Spain: Author.

■ If a non-English reference work is used as the source, give the title in the original language and, in brackets, the English translation.

29. Entry in an online reference work

> Graham, G. (2005). Behaviorism. In E. N. Zalta (Ed.), *The Stanford encyclopedia of philosophy* (Fall 2007 ed.). Retrieved from http://plato.stanford.edu/entries/behaviorism/

30. Entry in an online reference work, no author or editor

> Heuristic. (n.d.). In *Merriam-Webster's online dictionary* (11th ed.). Retrieved from http://www.m-w.com/dictionary/heuristic

■ If the online version refers to a print edition, include the edition number after the title.

8.03 Technical and Research Reports

Technical and research reports, like journal articles, usually cover original research but may or may not be peer reviewed. They are part of a body of literature sometimes referred to as *gray literature*, which "can serve a valuable supplementary role to formal publication, including additional resources, details, research methods and experimental techniques" ("Gray literature," 2006). Format references to technical and research reports as you would a book.

> Author, A. A. (1998). *Title of work* (Report No. xxx). Location: Publisher.

■ If the issuing organization assigned a number (e.g., report number, contract number, monograph number) to the report, give that number in parentheses immediately after the title.

- If you obtained a report from the U.S. Government Printing Office, list the publisher location and name as Washington, DC: Government Printing Office.

- For reports retrieved online, identify the publisher as part of the retrieval statement unless the publisher has been identified as the author: Retrieved from Agency name website: http://xxxxxxx

31. Corporate author, government report

U.S. Department of Health and Human Services, National Institutes of Health, National Heart, Lung, and Blood Institute. (2003). *Managing asthma: A guide for schools* (NIH Publication No. 02-2650). Retrieved from http://www.nhlbi.nih .gov/health/prof/lung/asthma/asth_sch.pdf

32. Corporate author, task force report filed online

American Psychological Association, Task Force on the Sexualization of Girls. (2007). *Report of the APA Task Force on the Sexualization of Girls.* Retrieved from http://www.apa.org/pi/wpo /sexualization.html

33. Authored report, from nongovernmental organization

Kessy, S. S. A., & Urio, F. M. (2006). *The contribution of microfinance institutions to poverty reduction in Tanzania* (Research Report No. 06.3). Retrieved from Research on Poverty Alleviation website: http://www.repoa.or.tz/documents _storage/Publications/Reports/06.3_Kessy_and _Urio.pdf

34. Report from institutional archive

McDaniel, J. E., & Miskel, C. G. (2002). *The effect of groups and individuals on national decision-making: Influence and domination in the reading policymaking environment* (CIERA Report 3-025). Retrieved from University of Michigan, Center for

> Improvement of Early Reading Achievement website: http://www.ciera.org/library/reports /inquiry-3/3-025/3-025.pdf

35. Issue brief

> Employee Benefit Research Institute. (1992, February). *Sources of health insurance and characteristics of the uninsured* (Issue Brief No. 123). Washington, DC: Author.

■ Use this form for issue briefs, working papers, and other corporate documents, with the appropriate document number for retrieval in parentheses.

8.04 Meetings and Symposia

Proceedings of meetings and symposia can be published in book or periodical form. To cite published proceedings from a book, use the same format as for a book or book chapter (see Example 39). To cite proceedings that are published regularly, use the same format as for a periodical (see Example 38). For contributions to symposia or for paper or poster presentations that have not been formally published, use the following templates.

Symposium:

> Contributor, A. A., Contributor, B. B., Contributor, C. C., & Contributor, D. D. (Year, Month). Title of contribution. In E. E. Chairperson (Chair), *Title of symposium*. Symposium conducted at the meeting of Organization Name, Location.

Paper presentation or poster session:

> Presenter, A. A. (Year, Month). *Title of paper or poster*. Paper or poster session presented at the meeting of Organization Name, Location.

■ For symposium contributions and paper or poster presentations that have not been formally published, give the month and year of the symposium or meeting in the reference.

36. Symposium contribution

Muellbauer, J. (2007, September). Housing, credit, and consumer expenditure. In S. C. Ludvigson (Chair), *Housing and consumer behavior.* Symposium conducted at the meeting of the Federal Reserve Bank of Kansas City, Jackson Hole, WY.

37. Conference paper abstract retrieved online

Liu, S. (2005, May). *Defending against business crises with the help of intelligent agent based early warning solutions.* Paper presented at the Seventh International Conference on Enterprise Information Systems, Miami, FL. Abstract retrieved from http://www.iceis.org/iceis2005 /abstracts_2005.htm

38. Proceedings published regularly online

Herculano-Houzel, S., Collins, C. E., Wong, P., Kaas, J. H., & Lent, R. (2008). The basic nonuniformity of the cerebral cortex. *Proceedings of the National Academy of Sciences, USA, 105,* 12593–12598. doi:10.1073/pnas.0805417105

39. Proceedings published in book form

Katz, I., Gabayan, K., & Aghajan, H. (2007). A multitouch surface using multiple cameras. In J. Blanc-Talon, W. Philips, D. Popescu, & P. Scheunders (Eds.), *Lecture Notes in Computer Science: Vol. 4678. Advanced Concepts for Intelligent Vision Systems* (pp. 97–108). doi: 10.1007/978-3-540-74607-2_9

8.05 Doctoral Dissertations and Master's Theses

Doctoral dissertations and master's theses can be retrieved from subscription databases, institutional archives, and personal websites. If the work is retrieved from ProQuest Dissertations and Theses database (whose index and abstracting sources include *Dissertation Abstracts International* [*DAI*] and *Master's Theses International,* both published by University Microforms International, and *American Doctoral Dissertations*, published by Association of Research Libraries) or another published source, include this information in the reference.

For a doctoral dissertation or master's thesis available from a database service, use the following reference template:

> Author, A. A. (2003). *Title of doctoral dissertation or master's thesis* (Doctoral dissertation or master's thesis). Retrieved from Name of database. (Accession or Order No.)

For an unpublished dissertation or thesis, use the following template:

> Author, A. A. (1978). *Title of doctoral dissertation or master's thesis* (Unpublished doctoral dissertation or master's thesis). Name of Institution, Location.

- Italicize the title of a doctoral dissertation or master's thesis.
- Identify the work as a doctoral dissertation or master's thesis in parentheses after the title.
- If the paper is available through a database, give the accession or order number in parentheses at the end of the reference.

40. Master's thesis, from a commercial database

> McNiel, D. S. (2006). *Meaning through narrative: A personal narrative discussing growing up with an*

alcoholic mother (Master's thesis). Available from ProQuest Dissertations and Theses database. (UMI No. 1434728)

41. Doctoral dissertation, from an institutional database

Adams, R. J. (1973). *Building a foundation for evaluation of instruction in higher education and continuing education* (Doctoral dissertation). Retrieved from http://www.ohiolink.edu/etd/

42. Doctoral dissertation, from the web

Bruckman, A. (1997). *MOOSE Crossing: Construction, community, and learning in a networked virtual world for kids* (Doctoral dissertation, Massachusetts Institute of Technology). Retrieved from http://www-static.cc.gatech.edu/~asb/thesis/

43. Doctoral dissertation, abstracted in *DAI*

Appelbaum, L. G. (2005). Three studies of human information processing: Texture amplification, motion representation, and figure-ground segregation. *Dissertation Abstracts International: Section B. Sciences and Engineering, 65*(10), 5428.

44. Doctoral thesis, from a university outside the United States

Carlbom, P. (2000). *Carbody and passengers in rail vehicle dynamics* (Doctoral thesis, Royal Institute of Technology, Stockholm, Sweden). Retrieved from http://urn.kb.se/resolve?urn=urn:nbn:se:kth:diva-3029

8.06 Reviews and Peer Commentary

Reviews of books, motion pictures, and other information or entertainment products are published in a variety of venues, including periodicals, websites, and blogs. Some publications will print author responses to a reviewer's criticism or multiple reviews of the same product.

> Reviewer, A. A. (2000). Title of review [Review of the book *Title of book*, by A. A. Author]. *Title of complete work, xx*, xxx–xxx.

- If the review is untitled, use the material in brackets as the title; retain the brackets to indicate that the material is a description of form and content, not a title.
- Identify the type of medium being reviewed in brackets (book, motion picture, television program, etc.).
- If the reviewed item is a book, include the author names after the title of the book, separated by a comma.
- If the reviewed item is a film, DVD, or other media, include the year of release after the title of the work, separated by a comma.

45. Review of a book

> Schatz, B. R. (2000, November 17). Learning by text or context? [Review of the book *The social life of information*, by J. S. Brown and P. Duguid]. *Science, 290*, 1304. doi:10.1126/science.290.5495.1304

46. Review of a video

> Axelman, A., & Shapiro, J. L. (2007). Does the solution warrant the problem? [Review of the DVD *Brief therapy with adolescents*, produced by the American Psychological Association, 2007]. *PsycCRITIQUES, 52*(51). doi:10.1037/a0009036

47. Review of a video game, no author

> [Review of the video game *BioShock,* produced by 2K Games, 2007]. (n.d.). Retrieved from http://www.whattheyplay.com/products/bioshock-for-xbox-360/?fm=3&ob=1&t=0#166

48. Peer commentary on an article

> Wolf, K. S. (2005). *The future for Deaf individuals is not that bleak* [Peer commentary on the paper "Decrease of Deaf potential in a mainstreamed

environment" by K. S. Wolf]. Retrieved from http://www.personalityresearch.org/papers/hall .html#wolf

8.07 Audiovisual Media

Audiovisual media include motion pictures; audio or television broadcasts (including podcasts); and static objects such as maps, artwork, or photos.

For a motion picture, use the following format:

> Producer, A. A. (Producer), & Director, B. B. (Director). (Year). *Title of motion picture* [Motion picture]. Country of Origin: Studio.

For a music recording, use the following format:

> Writer, A. (Copyright year). Title of song [Recorded by B. B. Artist if different from writer]. On *Title of album* [Medium of recording: CD, record, cassette, etc.] Location: Label. (Date of recording if different from song copyright date)

- List the primary contributors in the author position and use parentheses to identify their contribution.
- For an episode from a television or radio series, use the same format as for a chapter in a book, but list the script writer and director in the author position and the producer in the editor position.

49. Video

> American Psychological Association (Producer). (2000). *Responding therapeutically to patient expressions of sexual attraction* [DVD]. Available from http://www.apa.org/videos

50. Podcast

> Van Nuys, D. (Producer). (2007, December 19). *Shrink rap radio* [Audio podcast]. Retrieved from http://www.shrinkrapradio.com/

51. Single episode from a television series

Egan, D. (Writer), & Alexander, J. (Director). (2005). Failure to communicate [Television series episode]. In D. Shore (Executive producer), *House*. New York, NY: Fox Broadcasting.

52. Music recording

lang, k.d. (2008). Shadow and the frame. On *Watershed* [CD]. New York, NY: Nonesuch Records.

■ In text citations, include side and band or track numbers: "Shadow and the Frame" (lang, 2008, track 10).

53. Map retrieved online

Lewis County Geographic Information Services (Cartographer). (2002). Population density, 2000 U.S. Census [Demographic map]. Retrieved from http://www.co.lewis.wa.us/publicworks/maps /Demographics/census-popdens_2000.pdf

8.08 Data Sets, Software, Measurement Instruments, and Apparatus

This category includes raw data and tools that aid persons in performing a task such as data analysis or measurement. Reference entries are not necessary for standard software and programming languages, such as Microsoft Word or Excel, Java, Adobe Photoshop, and even SAS and SPSS. In text, give the proper name of the software, along with the version number. Do provide reference entries for specialized software or computer programs with limited distribution.

Rightsholder, A. A. (Year). Title of program (Version number) [Description of form]. Location: Name of producer.

or

> Rightsholder, A. A. (Year). Title of program [Description of form]. Retrieved from http://xxxx

- Do not italicize the names of software, programs, or languages.
- Do italicize the title of a data set.
- If an individual has proprietary rights to the software, name him or her as the author; otherwise, treat such references as unauthored works.
- In parentheses immediately after the title, identify the version number, if any.
- In brackets immediately after the title or version number, identify the source as a computer program, language, software, and so forth. Do not use a period between the title and the bracketed material.
- Give the location and name of the organization that produced the work, if applicable, in the publisher position. If the program can be downloaded or ordered from the web, give this information in the publisher position.
- For an apparatus patent, use the legal reference format (see Appendix 8.1).

54. Data set

> Pew Hispanic Center. (2004). *Changing channels and crisscrossing cultures: A survey of Latinos on the news media* [Data file and code book]. Retrieved from http://pewhispanic.org/datasets/

55. Measurement instrument

> Friedlander, M. L., Escudero, V., & Heatherington, L. (2002). E-SOFTA: System for observing family therapy alliances [Software and training videos]. Unpublished instrument. Retrieved from http://www.softa-soatif.com/

56. Software

> Comprehensive Meta-Analysis (Version 2) [Computer software]. Englewood, NJ: Biostat.

57. Apparatus

> Eyelink II [Apparatus and software]. (2004). Mississauga, Ontario, Canada: SR Research.

8.09 Unpublished and Informally Published Works

Unpublished work includes work that is in progress, has been submitted for publication, or has been completed but not submitted for publication. This category also includes work that has not been formally published but is available on a personal or institutional website, an electronic archive such as ERIC, or a preprint archive.

> Author, A. A. (Year). *Title of manuscript.* Unpublished manuscript [or "Manuscript submitted for publication," or "Manuscript in preparation"].

- If the work is available on an electronic archive, give this information at the end.
- Update your references frequently prior to publication of your work; refer to the final published version of sources when possible.

58. Unpublished manuscript with a university cited

> Blackwell, E., & Conrod, P. J. (2003). *A five-dimensional measure of drinking motives.* Unpublished manuscript, Department of Psychology, University of British Columbia, Vancouver, Canada.

59. Manuscript in progress or submitted for publication

> Ting, J. Y., Florsheim, P., & Huang, W. (2008). *Mental health help-seeking in ethnic minority populations: A theoretical perspective.* Manuscript submitted for publication.

- Do not give the name of the journal or publisher to which the manuscript has been submitted.
- Treat a manuscript accepted for publication but not yet published as an in-press reference (see Example 6).

- Use the same format for a draft or work in progress, but substitute the words Manuscript in preparation for the final sentence. Use the year of the draft you read (not *in preparation*) in the text citation.

60. Unpublished raw data from study, untitled work

Bordi, F., & LeDoux, J. E. (1993). [Auditory response latencies in rat auditory cortex]. Unpublished raw data.

61. Informally published or self-archived work

Mitchell, S. D. (2000). *The import of uncertainty.* Retrieved from http://philsci-archive.pitt.edu /archive/00000162/

This work was later published in a journal and would now be referenced as follows:

Mitchell, S. D. (2007). The import of uncertainty. *The Pluralist, 2*(1), 58–71.

62. Informally published or self-archived work, from ERIC

Kubota, K. (2007). *"Soaking" model for learning: Analyzing Japanese learning/teaching process from a socio-historical perspective.* Retrieved from ERIC database. (ED498566)

8.10 Archival Documents and Collections

Archival sources include letters, unpublished manuscripts, limited-circulation brochures and pamphlets, inhouse institutional and corporate documents, clippings, and other documents, as well as such nontext materials as photographs and apparatus, that are in the personal possession of an author, form part of an institutional collection, or are stored in an archive such as the Archives of the History of American Psychology at the University of Akron or the APA Archives.

Author, A. A. (Year, Month Day). *Title of material.* [Description of material]. Name of Collection (Call

> number, Box number, File name or number, etc.). Name of Repository, Location.

- This general format may be modified for collections requiring more or less specific information to locate materials, for different types of collections, or for additional descriptive information (e.g., a translation of a letter). Authors may choose to list correspondence from their own personal collections, but correspondence from other private collections should be listed only with the permission of the collector.
- As with any reference, the purpose is to direct the reader to the source, despite the fact that only a single copy of the document may be available and the reader may have some difficulty actually seeing a copy.
- Include as much information as is needed to help locate the item with reasonable ease within the repository. For items from collections with detailed finding aids, the name of the collection may be sufficient; for items from collections without finding aids, more information (e.g., call number, box number, file name or number) may be necessary to help locate the item.
- If several letters are cited from the same collection, list the collection as a reference and provide specific identifying information (author, recipient, and date) for each letter in the in-text citations.
- Use square brackets to indicate information that does not appear on the document. Use question marks to indicate uncertainty regarding names and dates; use ca. (circa, not italicized) to indicate estimated dates (see Example 67).
- For interviews and oral histories, list the interviewee as the author. Include the interviewer's name in the description.
- If a publication of limited circulation is available in libraries, the reference may be formatted as usual for published material, without the archival source.

63. Letter from a repository

> Frank, L. K. (1935, February 4). [Letter to Robert M. Ogden]. Rockefeller Archive Center (GEB series 1.3, Box 371, Folder 3877), Tarrytown, NY.

64. Letter from private collection

> Zacharius, G. P. (1953, August 15). [Letter to William Rickel (W. Rickel, Trans.)]. Copy in possession of Hendrika Vande Kemp.

65. Collection of letters from an archive

> Allport, G. W. (1930–1967). Correspondence. Gordon W. Allport Papers (HUG 4118.10). Harvard University Archives, Cambridge, MA.

In-text citations of specific letters:

> (Allport, G. W., 1930–1967, Allport to E. G. Boring, March 1, 1939)

> (Allport, G. W., 1930–1967, E. G. Boring to Allport, December 26, 1937)

■ Note that Examples 63 and 65 refer to archival materials that can be recovered and thus include full reference list details that allow the reader to find them. Private letters and correspondence that are not easily retrievable are considered personal communications and are cited only in text (see section 7.21).

66. Unpublished papers, lectures from an archive or personal collection

> Berliner, A. (1959). *Notes for a lecture on reminiscences of Wundt and Leipzig.* Anna Berliner Memoirs (Box M50). Archives of the History of American Psychology, University of Akron, Akron, OH.

67. Archival/historical source for which the author and/or date is known or is reasonably certain but not stated on the document

> [Allport, A.?]. [ca. 1937]. *Marion Taylor today—by the biographer.* Unpublished manuscript, Marion Taylor Papers. Schlesinger Library, Radcliffe College, Cambridge, MA.

68. Archival source with corporate author

Subcommittee on Mental Hygiene Personnel in School Programs. (1949, November 5–6). *Meeting of Subcommittee on Mental Hygiene Personnel in School Programs*. David Shakow Papers (M1360). Archives of the History of American Psychology, University of Akron, Akron, OH.

69. Interview recorded and available in an archive

Smith, M. B. (1989, August 12). Interview by C. A. Kiesler [Tape recording]. President's Oral History Project, American Psychological Association. APA Archives, Washington, DC.

70. Transcription of a recorded interview, no recording available

Sparkman, C. F. (1973). *An oral history with Dr. Colley F. Sparkman/Interviewer: Orley B. Caudill*. Mississippi Oral History Program (Vol. 289), University of Southern Mississippi, Hattiesburg.

71. Newspaper article, historical, in an archive or personal collection

Psychoanalysis institute to open. (1948, September 18). [Clipping from an unidentified Dayton, OH newspaper]. Copy in possession of author.

72. Historical publication of limited circulation

Sci-Art Publishers. (1935). *Sci-Art Publications* [Brochure]. Cambridge, MA: Author. A. A. Roback Papers (HUGFP 104.50, Box 2, Folder "Miscellaneous Psychological Materials"). Harvard University Archives, Cambridge, MA.

73. Photographs

[Photographs of Robert M. Yerkes]. (ca. 1917–1954). Robert Mearns Yerkes Papers (Box 137,

Folder 2292). Manuscripts and Archives, Yale University Library, New Haven, CT.

8.11 Internet Message Boards, Electronic Mailing Lists, and Other Online Communities

The Internet offers several options for people around the world to sponsor and join discussions devoted to particular subjects. These options include blogs, newsgroups, online forums and discussion groups, and electronic mailing lists. (The last are often referred to as *listservs*. However, LISTSERV is a trademarked name for a particular software program; *electronic mailing list* is the appropriate generic term.)

Author, A. A. (Year, Month Day). Title of post [Description of form]. Retrieved from http:xxxx

- If the author's full name is available, list the last name first followed by initials. If only a screen name is available, use the screen name.
- Provide the exact date of the posting.
- Follow the date with the subject line of the message (also referred to as the "thread"); do not italicize it. Provide a description of the message in brackets after the title.
- Include the information "Retrieved from" followed by the URL where the message can be retrieved. Include the name of the list to which the message was posted, if this information is not part of the URL.
- Provide the address for the archived version of the message.

74. Message posted to a newsgroup, online forum, or discussion group

Rampersad, T. (2005, June 8). Re: Traditional knowledge and traditional cultural expressions [Online forum comment]. Retrieved from http://www.wipo.int/roller/comments/ipisforum/Weblog/theme_eight_how_can_cultural#comments

75. Message posted to an electronic mailing list

Smith, S. (2006, January 5). Re: Disputed estimates of IQ [Electronic mailing list message]. Retrieved from http://tech.groups.yahoo.com /group/ForensicNetwork/message/670

76. Blog post

PZ Myers. (2007, January 22). The unfortunate prerequisites and consequences of partitioning your mind [Web log post]. Retrieved from http://scienceblogs.com/pharyngula/2007/01/the _unfortunate_prerequisites.php

A blog comment would be referenced as follows:

MiddleKid. (2007, January 22). Re: The unfortunate prerequisites and consequences of partitioning your mind [Web log comment]. Retrieved from http://scienceblogs.com/pharyngula/2007/01/the _unfortunate_prerequisites.php

■ In the second example a screen name is used for the author name. The author has adopted a nickname, or screen name, to use when posting comments to this web log.

77. Video blog post

Norton, R. (2006, November 4). How to train a cat to operate a light switch [Video file]. Retrieved from http://www.youtube.com/watch?v=Vja83KLQXZs

Appendix 8.1: References to Legal Materials

Legal periodicals and APA journals differ in the placement and format of references. The main difference is that legal periodicals cite references in footnotes, whereas APA journals locate all references, including references to legal materials, in the reference list. For most references, use APA format as described in this chapter. References to legal materials, however, which include court decisions, statutes, other legislative materials, and various secondary sources, are more useful to the reader if they provide the information in the conventional format of legal citations. Some examples of references and citations to court cases, statutes, and other legislative materials appear in this appendix along with guidelines for their preparation. For more information on preparing these and other kinds of legal references, consult the latest edition of *The Bluebook: A Uniform System of Citation* (*Bluebook*; 18th ed., 2005), which is the source for the legal citation style that follows.

Ensure that your legal references are accurate and contain all of the information necessary to enable a reader to locate the material being referenced. Consult law librarians to verify that your legal references (a) contain the information necessary for retrieval and (b) reflect the current status of the legal authority cited to avoid the possibility of relying on a case that has been overturned on appeal or on legislation that has been significantly amended or repealed.

A8.01 General Forms

A reference form is provided in each of the following sections. For the most part, each reference form for statutes and other legislation includes (a) a popular or formal title or name of the legislation and (b) the citation, either to the published compilation of legislative materials where the legislation is codified (e.g., a specific numbered section of a specific volume of the *United States Code*), including the statutory compilation's publication date in parentheses, or the identifying label for the legislation assigned by the enacting body during the particular legislative session (e.g., a specific section of an act identified by its public law number).

A typical reference form for court decisions includes (a) the title or name of the case (usually one party vs. another); (b) the citation, usually to a volume and page of one of the various sets of books (called *reporters*, which usually contain decisions of courts in particular political divisions, or *jurisdictions*) where published cases can be found (e.g., the *Federal Reporter, Second Series*); and finally, (c) the precise jurisdiction of the court writing the decision (e.g., the New York Court of Appeals), in parentheses, including the date of the decision.

For both legislation and court decisions, the citation may be followed by certain additional descriptive information that pertains to the content of the legislation or court decision, the history of the legislation or court decision (e.g., later appeals of court decisions or later amendments to legislation), or other sources from which the legislation or court citation may be retrieved. Authors are encouraged to consult the *Bluebook* for the proper format for such additional information. Follow the *Bluebook* closely for correct abbreviation style. Some examples of the more common abbreviations that appear in APA journals are shown here.

Cong.	U.S. Congress
H.R.	House of Representatives
S.	Senate
Reg.	Regulation
Res.	Resolution
F.	*Federal Reporter*
F.2d	*Federal Reporter, Second Series*
F.3d	*Federal Reporter, Third Series*
F. Supp.	*Federal Supplement*
U.S.C.	*United States Code*
Cong. Rec.	*Congressional Record*
Fed. Reg.	*Federal Register*

A8.02 Text Citations of Legal Materials

Although the reference format for legal materials differs from that of other kinds of works cited in APA publications, the text citations are formed in the same way and serve the same purpose. As for works with no identified author (see section 7.16), give the first few words of the reference list entry and date; that is, give enough information in the text citation to enable the reader to locate the entry in the reference list quickly and easily. Examples of text citations and reference entries for specific kinds of legal materials are given in the following sections.

A8.03 Court Decisions (*Bluebook* Rule 10)

In text, cite the name of the case (italicized) and the year of the decision. If two or more years are given, cite those years as well. Court cases often have several years, each of which reflects a specific stage in the case's history. Giving only one date could give the impression that only a single point in the case's history is being cited or might mislead a reader as to the timing of the case.

Reference form for cases:

> Name v. Name, Volume Source Page (Court Date).

Abbreviate the published source (if any), court, and date as specified in the *Bluebook*.

1. Sample reference list entry to a case

> Lessard v. Schmidt, 349 F. Supp. 1078 (E.D. Wis. 1972).

Text citation:

> *Lessard v. Schmidt* (1972)

> (*Lessard v. Schmidt,* 1972)

Explanation: This decision was rendered by the federal district court for the Eastern District of Wisconsin in

1972. It appears in volume 349 of the *Federal Supplement* and starts on page 1078 of that volume.

2. Sample reference list entry to an appealed case

> Durflinger v. Artiles, 563 F. Supp. 322 (D. Kan. 1981), *aff'd,* 727 F.2d 888 (10th Cir. 1984).

Text citation:

> *Durflinger v. Artiles* (1981/1984)

Explanation: This decision was rendered by the federal district court for the District of Kansas in 1981. On appeal, the decision was affirmed by the 10th Circuit Court of Appeals in 1984. Consult the *Bluebook* for the proper forms to signal the various stages in a case's history.

Unpublished cases:

3. Sample reference to an unreported decision

> Gilliard v. Oswald, No. 76-2109 (2d Cir. Mar. 16, 1977).

Explanation: The docket number and the court are provided. The opinion was announced on March 16, 1977. To cite to a particular page of a *slip opinion* (opinion that is not published in a case reporter but is separately printed), use the form slip op. at [page number].

Alternative: You may cite unreported cases found on electronic databases, such as LEXIS or Westlaw, instead of citing them to slip opinions. Give the name of the database, a record number if available, and enough information for the reader to find the case. Precede screen page numbers, if assigned, with an asterisk to distinguish them from the page number of the slip opinion; paragraph numbers, if assigned, should be preceded by a paragraph symbol.

With record number:

> Dougherty v. Royal Zenith Corp., No. 88-8666, 1991 U.S. Dist. LEXIS 10807, at *2 (E.D. Pa. July 31, 1991).

With no record number:

> Gustin v. Mathews, No. 76-7-C5 (D. Kan. Jan. 31, 1977) (LEXIS, Genfed library, Dist file).

Note: If the case is not available as a slip opinion or on-line, consult the *Bluebook* for other reference formats.

Court cases at the trial level:

4. Sample reference to a state trial court opinion

> Casey v. Pennsylvania-American Water Co., 12 Pa. D. & C.4th 168 (C.P. Washington County 1991).

Explanation: This decision was rendered by the Court of Common Pleas in Washington County, Pennsylvania, in 1991. (The Court of Common Pleas is the name of most of the trial-level courts in Pennsylvania. In other states, the trial-level courts are called *superior courts* or *supreme courts*, which can be confusing because one usually thinks of the supreme court as the highest court in any particular jurisdiction and not as the lowest. Authors should check the *Bluebook* for a listing of each jurisdiction's particular court structure.) The decision can be located in *Pennsylvania District and County Reports, Fourth Series,* beginning on page 168 of that volume.

5. Sample reference to a federal district court opinion

> Davis v. Monsanto Co., 627 F. Supp. 418 (S.D. W. Va. 1986).

Explanation: The opinion was rendered in the federal district court for the Southern District of West Virginia and was decided in 1986. It appears in volume 627 of the *Federal Supplement* and starts on page 418 of that volume.

Court cases at the appellate level:

6. Sample reference to a case appealed to a state supreme court

> Compton v. Commonwealth, 239 Va. 312, 389 S.E.2d 460 (1990).

Explanation: This opinion was written by the Virginia Supreme Court in 1990. It can be found in volume 239 of the *Virginia Reports*, which publishes the state's supreme court decisions, starting on page 312. There is a parallel citation to volume 389 of the *South Eastern Reporter, Second Series*, starting on page 460. A reporter prints cases; the *South Eastern Reporter* is a regional reporter containing cases from several states in the southeastern section of the country.

7. Sample reference to a case appealed to a state court of appeals

> Texas v. Morales, 826 S.W.2d 201 (Tex. Ct. App. 1992).

Explanation: This opinion was rendered by the Texas Court of Appeals in 1992 and can be found in volume 826 of the *South Western Reporter, Second Series*, starting on page 201.

8. Sample references to cases decided by the U.S. Supreme Court

> Brown v. Board of Educ., 347 U.S. 483 (1954).

> Maryland v. Craig, 110 S. Ct. 3160 (1990).

Explanation: Each of these cases was decided by the U.S. Supreme Court. The first citation is to the *United States Reports.* Such a citation is given when the appropriate volume of the *United States Reports* is available. The second citation is to the *Supreme Court Reporter.* Use this source when the volume of the *United States Reports* in which the case will appear has not yet been published.

A8.04 Statutes (*Bluebook* Rule 12)

In text, give the popular or official name of the act (if any) and the year of the act. In the reference list entry, include the source and section number of the statute, and in parentheses, give the publication date of the statutory compilation, which may be different from the year in the name of the act.

Reference form for statutes:

> Name of Act, Volume Source § xxx (year).

Abbreviate the source as specified in the *Bluebook*. A few states use chapter or article numbers instead of section numbers; use abbreviations or symbols as shown in the *Bluebook*.

9. Sample reference to a statute

> Mental Health Systems Act, 42 U.S.C. § 9401 (1988).

Text citation:

> Mental Health Systems Act (1988)

> Mental Health Systems Act of 1988

10. Sample reference to a statute in a state code

> Mental Care and Treatment Act, 4 Kan. Stat. Ann. §§ 59-2901-2941 (1983 & Supp. 1992).

Explanation: This Kansas act can be found in codified version between sections 2901 and 2941 in Chapter 59 of volume 4 of the 1983 edition of *Kansas Statutes Annotated.* Two amendments to the act and additional references are provided in the 1992 supplement for the *Kansas Statutes Annotated.* If you are discussing a particular provision of the law, cite the particular section in which the provision appeared (e.g., § 59-2903). *Ann.* stands for *Annotated,* which refers to the version of the Kansas statutory compilation containing summarized cases interpreting particular sections of the statute.

11. Sample reference to a statute in a federal code

> Americans With Disabilities Act of 1990, 42 U.S.C.A. § 12101 *et seq.* (West 1993).

Explanation: This act can be located beginning at section 12101 of title 42 of the *United States Code Annotated,* which is the unofficial version of the *United States Code* (the official statutory compilation of the laws enacted by Congress). *Et seq.* is a Latin phrase meaning "and following" and is a shorthand way of showing that the act covers not just the initial section cited but also others that follow the initial section. The text in parentheses indicates that the *United States Code Annotated* is published by West Publishing and that 1993 is the publication date of the volume in which the cited sections can be found. Citing to U.S.C., U.S.C.A., or U.S.C.S. is the preferred method of citing legislation, because codified legislation is usually easier to work with and retrieve than is a session law, the form of legislation before it is codified. A session law citation is constructed as follows:

Americans With Disabilities Act of 1990, Pub. L. No. 101-336, § 2, 104 Stat. 328 (1991).

Explanation: The citation is to the version of the act in its uncodified form. The act was the 336th public law enacted by the 101st Congress. Section 2 is the particular section of the act cited (§ 2 happens to correspond to § 12101 of 42 U.S.C.A., which is where § 2 was ultimately codified). The text of the section cited can also be found in the official compilation of uncodified session laws, called *United States Statutes at Large* (abbreviated *Stat.*) at volume 104, p. 328. Volume 104 of the *United States Statutes at Large* was published in 1991.

A8.05 Legislative Materials (*Bluebook* Rule 13)

For testimony and hearings, bills and resolutions, and reports and documents, provide in text the title or number (or other descriptive information) and the date.

Form for testimony at federal hearings and for full hearings:

Title, xxx Cong. (date).

12. Sample reference for federal testimony

> *RU486: The import ban and its effect on medical research: Hearings before the Subcommittee on Regulation, Business Opportunities, and Energy, of the House Committee on Small Business,* 101st Cong. 35 (1990) (testimony of Ronald Chesemore).

Text citation:

> *RU486: The Import Ban* (1990)
>
> (*RU486: The Import Ban,* 1990)

Explanation: This testimony was given before a subcommittee of the U.S. House of Representatives during the second session of the 101st Congress and can be located beginning on page 35 of the official pamphlet that documents the hearing. In the reference, always include the entire subject-matter title as it appears on the cover of the pamphlet, the bill number (if any), the subcommittee name (if any), and the committee name. If you are citing an entire hearing, certain adjustments to the citation should be made, as in Example 13.

13. Sample reference for a full federal hearing

> *Urban America's need for social services to strengthen families: Hearing before the Subcommittee on Human Resources of the Committee on Ways and Means, House of Representatives,* 102d Cong. 1 (1992).

Text citation:

> *Urban America's Need* (1992)
>
> (*Urban America's Need,* 1992)

Explanation: This hearing was held in 1992 in the U.S. House of Representatives during the 102d Congress. The hearing begins on page 1 of the official pamphlet that was prepared after the hearing.

14. Form for unenacted federal bills and resolutions

> Title [if relevant], bill or resolution number, xxx Cong. (year).

The number should be preceded by *H.R.* (House of Representatives) or *S.* (Senate), depending on the source of the unenacted bill or resolution.

Reference list entry:

> S. 5936, 102d Cong. § 4 (1992).

Text citation:

> Senate Bill 5936 (1992)
>
> (S. 5936, 1992)

15. Sample references to unenacted federal bills

> Equitable Health Care for Severe Mental Illnesses Act of 1993, H.R. 1563, 103d Cong. (1993).
>
> Equitable Health Care for Severe Mental Illnesses Act of 1993, S. 671, 103d Cong. (1993).

Explanation: The first example is to a bill created in the U.S. House of Representatives during the 103d Congress; it was assigned the bill number 1563. The second example is the Senate's version of the same bill.

16. Form for enacted federal bills and resolutions

> xx. Res. xxx, xxx Cong., Volume Source page (year) (enacted).

Reference list entry:

> S. Res. 107, 103d Cong., 139 Cong. Rec. 5826 (1993) (enacted).

Text citation:

> Senate Resolution 107 (1993)
>
> (S. Res. 107., 1993)

Explanation: This resolution by the Senate is numbered 107 and is reported in volume 139 of the *Congressional Record* on page 5826. Note that enacted bills and joint resolutions are laws and should be cited as statutes. Enacted simple or concurrent resolutions should follow this format.

17. Form for federal reports (Rep.) and documents (Doc.)

xx. Rep. No. xx-xxx (year).

As with bills, report numbers should be preceded by *H.R.* or *S.* as appropriate. The report number is composed of the year of the Congress followed by a hyphen and the number of the report, and ending with the calendar year.

Reference list entry:

S. Rep. No. 102-114, at 7 (1991).

Text citation:

Senate Report No. 102-114 (1991)

(S. Rep. No. 102-114, 1991)

Explanation: This report was submitted to the Senate by the Senate Committee on Labor and Human Resources concerning the Protection and Advocacy for Mentally Ill Individuals Amendments Act of 1991. The reference is to material that starts on page 7 of that document.

A8.06 Administrative and Executive Materials (*Bluebook* Rule 14)

For rules and regulations, advisory opinions, and executive orders, provide in text the title or number (or other descriptive information) and the date.

18. Form for federal regulation

Title/Number, Volume Source § xxx (year).

Reference list entries:

> FDA Prescription Drug Advertising Rule, 21 C.F.R. § 202.1 (2006).

> Adoption and Foster Care Analysis and Reporting System, 73 Fed. Reg. 82,082 (proposed Jan. 11, 2008) (to be codified at 45 C.F.R. pt. 1355).

Text citations:

> FDA Prescription Drug Advertising Rule (2006)

> (Adoption and Foster Care Analysis and Reporting System, 2008)

Explanation: The first rule was codified in 2006 in volume 21 of the *Code of Federal Regulations* (the official regulatory code) as section 202.1. The second rule was proposed and published in the *Federal Register* before being officially codified; the parenthetical information is a cross-reference (indicated in the entry in the *Register*) to the section of the *Code of Federal Regulations* where the proposed rule will be codified.

19. Form for executive order

> Exec. Order No. xxxxx, 3 C.F.R. Page (year).

Reference list entry:

> Exec. Order No. 11,609, 3 C.F.R. 586 (1971–1975), *reprinted as amended in* 3 U.S.C. 301 app. at 404-07 (1994).

Text citation:

> Executive Order No. 11,609 (1994)

> (Executive Order No. 11,609, 1994)

Explanation: Executive orders are reported in title 3 of the *Code of Federal Regulations*; this one appears on page 586. Provide a parallel citation to the *United States Code* (U.S.C.) or, if U.S.C. is unavailable, to the *United States Code Service* (U.S.C.S.).

A8.07 Patents

In text, give the patent number and the issue date (not application date) of the patent. In the reference list entry, include the inventor(s) to whom the patent is issued and the official source from which the patent information can be retrieved.

Reference list entry:

> Smith, I. M. (1988). *U.S. Patent No. 123,445.* Washington, DC: U.S. Patent and Trademark Office.

Text citation:

> U.S. Patent No. 123,445 (1988)

> (U.S. Patent No. 123,445, 1988)

Explanation: This patent was issued in 1988. I. M. Smith is the inventor who holds the patent right. The patent number is a unique identifying code given to every patent. In this reference example, the patent number represents a utility patent because there is no letter prefix. If this were a nonutility patent, such as a design patent (coded with a *D*), the patent number in the reference and citation would be D123,445.

Appendix: Checklist for Manuscript Submission

Numbers following entries refer to relevant section numbers in the *Publication Manual* (APA, 2010; this checklist can also be found online at http://www.apa.org/journals).

▨ Checklist for Manuscript Submission

Format

☐ Have you checked the journal's website for instructions to authors regarding specific formatting requirements for submission (8.03)?

☐ Is the entire manuscript—including quotations, references, author note, content footnotes, and figure captions—double-spaced (8.03)? Is the manuscript neatly prepared (8.03)?

☐ Are the margins at least 1 in. (2.54 cm; 8.03)?

☐ Are the title page, abstract, references, appendices, author note, content footnotes, tables, and figures on separate pages (with only one table or figure per page)? Are the figure captions on the same page as the figures? Are manuscript elements ordered in sequence, with the text pages between the abstract and the references (8.03)?

▪ Checklist for Manuscript Submission (continued)

☐ Are all pages numbered in sequence, starting with the title page (8.03)?

Title Page and Abstract

☐ Is the title no more than 12 words (2.01)?

☐ Does the byline reflect the institution or institutions where the work was conducted (2.02)?

☐ Does the title page include the running head, article title, byline, and date, and author note (8.03)? (Note, however, that some publishers prefer that you include author identification information only in the cover letter. Check with your publisher and follow the recommended format.)

☐ Does the abstract range between 150 and 250 words (2.04)? (Note, however, that the abstract word limit changes periodically. Check http://www.apa.org/journals for updates to the APA abstract word limit.)

Paragraphs and Headings

☐ Is each paragraph longer than a single sentence but not longer than one manuscript page (3.08)?

☐ Do the levels of headings accurately reflect the organization of the paper (3.02–3.03)?

☐ Do all headings of the same level appear in the same format (3.02–3.03)?

Abbreviations

☐ Are unnecessary abbreviations eliminated and necessary ones explained (4.22–4.23)?

☐ Are abbreviations in tables and figures explained in the table notes and figure captions or legends (4.23)?

Mathematics and Statistics

☐ Are Greek letters and all but the most common mathematical symbols identified in the manuscript (4.45–4.49)?

☐ Are all non-Greek letters that are used as statistical symbols for algebraic variables in italics (4.45)?

Units of Measurement

☐ Are metric equivalents for all nonmetric units provided (except measurements of time, which have no metric equivalents; see 4.39)?

☐ Are all metric and nonmetric units with numeric values (except some measurements of time) abbreviated (4.27, 4.40)?

References

☐ Are references cited both in text and in the reference list (6.11–6.21)?

☐ Do the text citations and reference list entries agree both in spelling and in date (6.11–6.21)?

☐ Are journal titles in the reference list spelled out fully (6.29)?

☐ Are the references (both in the parenthetical text citations and in the reference list) ordered alphabetically by the authors' surnames (6.16, 6.25)?

☐ Are inclusive page numbers for all articles or chapters in books provided in the reference list (7.01, 7.02)?

☐ Are references to studies included in your meta-analysis preceded by an asterisk (6.26)?

■ Checklist for Manuscript Submission (continued)

Notes and Footnotes

☐ Is the departmental affiliation given for each author in the author note (2.03)?

☐ Does the author note include both the author's current affiliation if it is different from the byline affiliation and a current address for correspondence (2.03)?

☐ Does the author note disclose special circumstances about the article (portions presented at a meeting, student paper as basis for the article, report of a longitudinal study, relationship that may be perceived as a conflict of interest; 2.03)?

☐ In the text, are all footnotes indicated, and are footnote numbers correctly located (2.12)?

Tables and Figures

☐ Does every table column, including the stub column, have a heading (5.13, 5.19)?

☐ Have all vertical table rules been omitted (5.19)?

☐ Are all tables referred to in text (5.19)?

☐ Are the elements in the figures large enough to remain legible after the figure has been reduced to the width of a journal column or page (5.22, 5.25)?

☐ Is lettering in a figure no smaller than 8 points and no larger than 14 points (5.25)?

☐ Are the figures being submitted in a file format acceptable to the publisher (5.30)?

☐ Has the figure been prepared at a resolution sufficient to produce a high-quality image (5.25)?

☐ Are all figures numbered consecutively with Arabic numerals (5.30)?

☐ Are all figures and tables mentioned in the text and numbered in the order in which they are mentioned (5.05)?

Copyright and Quotations

☐ Is written permission to use previously published text, tests or portions of tests, tables, or figures enclosed with the manuscript (6.10)?

☐ Are page or paragraph numbers provided in text for all quotations (6.03, 6.05)?

Submitting the Manuscript

☐ Is the journal editor's contact information current (8.03)?

☐ Is a cover letter included with the manuscript? Does the letter

    ☐ include the author's postal address, e-mail address, telephone number, and fax number for future correspondence?

    ☐ state that the manuscript is original, not previously published, and not under concurrent consideration elsewhere?

    ☐ inform the journal editor of the existence of any similar published manuscripts written by the author (8.03, Figure 8.1)?

    ☐ mention any supplemental material you are submitting for the online version of your article?

References

American Psychiatric Association. (2000). *Diagnostic and statistical manual of mental disorders* (4th ed., text rev.). Washington, DC: Author.

American Psychological Association. (2004). Guidelines for psychological practice with older adults. *American Psychologist, 59,* 236–260. doi:10.1037/0003-066X.59.4.236

American Psychological Association. (2010). *Publication manual of the American Psychological Association* (6th ed.). Washington, DC: Author.

American Psychological Association, Committee on Lesbian, Gay, and Bisexual Concerns Joint Task Force on Guidelines for Psychotherapy With Lesbian, Gay, and Bisexual Clients. (2000). *Guidelines for psychotherapy with lesbian, gay, and bisexual clients.* Washington, DC: Author. Retrieved from http://www.apa.org/pi/lgbc/guidelines.html

American Psychological Association, Presidential Task Force on the Assessment of Age-Consistent

Memory Decline and Dementia. (1998). *Guidelines for the evaluation of dementia and age-related cognitive decline*. Washington, DC: Author. Retrieved from http://www.apa.org/practice/dementia.html

APA Publications and Communications Board Working Group on Journal Article Reporting Standards. (2008). Reporting standards for research in psychology: Why do we need them? What might they be? *American Psychologist, 63*, 839–851. doi:10.1037/0003-066X.63.9.839

The bluebook: A uniform system of citation (18th ed.). (2005). Cambridge, MA: Harvard Law Review Association.

Devlin, J. T., & Poldrack, R. A. (2007). In praise of tedious anatomy. *NeuroImage, 37*, 1033–1041. doi:10.1016/j.neuroimage.2006.09.055

Gay & Lesbian Alliance Against Defamation. (2007). *GLAAD media reference guide* (7th ed.). Retrieved from http://www.glaad.org/media/guide/

Gray literature. (2006). In *Crossref glossary* (Version 1.0). Retrieved from http://www.crossref.org/02publishers/glossary.html

Hegarty, P., & Buechel, C. (2006). Androcentric reporting of gender differences in APA articles, 1965–2004. *Review of General Psychology, 10*, 377–389. doi:10.1037/1089-2680.10.4.377

Hyde, J. S. (2005). The gender similarities hypothesis. *American Psychologist, 60*, 581–592. doi:10.1037/0003-066X.60.6.581

Kasdorf, W. E. (Ed.). (2003). *The Columbia guide to digital publishing*. New York, NY: Columbia University Press.

Knatterud, M. E. (1991, February). Writing with the patient in mind: Don't add insult to injury. *American Medical Writers Association Journal, 6*, 10–17.

Merriam-Webster's collegiate dictionary (11th ed.). (2005). Springfield, MA: Merriam-Webster.

Meyer, W., Bockting, W. O., Cohen-Kettenis, P., Coleman, E., DiCeglie, D., Devor, H., ...Wheeler, C. C. (2001). The Harry Benjamin International Gender Dysphoria Association's standards of care for gender identity disorders, sixth version. *Journal of Psychology & Human Sexuality, 13*(1), 1–30. doi:10.1300/J056v13n01_01

Mildenberger, P., Eichenberg, M., & Martin, E. (2002). Introduction to the DICOM standard. *European Radiology, 12,* 920–927. doi:10.1007/s003300101100

National Lesbian & Gay Journalists Association. (2005). *Stylebook supplement on LGBT terminology.* Retrieved from http://www.nlgja.org/resources/stylebook.html

Picton, T. W., Benton, S., Berg, P., Donchin, E., Hillyard, S. A., Johnson, R. J., . . .Taylor, M. J. (2000). Guidelines for using human event-related potentials to study cognition: Recording standards and publication criteria. *Psychophysiology, 37,* 127–152. doi:10.1111/1469-8986.3720127

Rappaport, J. (1977). *Community psychology: Values, research and action.* New York, NY: Holt, Rinehart & Winston.

Schaie, K. W. (1993). Ageist language in psychological research. *American Psychologist, 48,* 49–51. doi:10.1037/0003-066X.48.1.49

University of Kansas, Research and Training Center on Independent Living. (2008). *Guidelines for reporting and writing about people with disabilities.* Lawrence, KS: Author.

VandenBos, G. R. (Ed.). (2007). *APA dictionary of psychology.* Washington, DC: American Psychological Association.

Wainer, H. (1997). Improving tabular displays: With NAEP tables as examples and inspirations. *Journal of Educational and Behavioral Statistics, 22*, 1–30.

Webster's third new international dictionary, unabridged. (2002). Springfield, MA: Merriam-Webster.

Index

Numbers in bold refer to section numbers.

The Sixth Edition of the
Publication Manual
of the **American Psychological Association**®

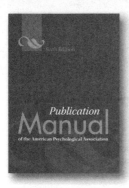

Publication
Manual
of the American Psychological Association

2010. 272 pages.

Paperback
ISBN 978-1-4338-0561-5

Hardcover
ISBN 978-1-4338-0559-2

Lay-Flat Spiral Binding
ISBN 978-1-4338-0562-2

THE DEFINITIVE GUIDE

The *Publication Manual* is the style manual of choice for writers, editors, students, and educators. Although it is specifically designed to help writers in the behavioral sciences and social sciences, anyone who writes non-fiction prose can benefit from its guidance.

THOROUGHLY REVISED

The newly revised Sixth Edition has been thoroughly rethought, reorganized, and rewritten.

EASIER TO USE

The Sixth Edition is the most user-friendly *Publication Manual* the APA has ever produced. You will be able to find answers to your questions faster than ever before.

PACKED WITH INFORMATION AND EXAMPLES

When you need advice on how to present information, including text, data, and graphics, for publication in any type of format—such as college and university papers, professional journals, presentations for colleagues, and online publication—you will find the advice you're looking for in the *Publication Manual*.

INCLUDES ONLINE FEATURES

When you purchase the *Publication Manual*, you are purchasing more than a book. You are also gaining access to an extensive website totally devoted to your writing concerns. The site is updated regularly, so the latest information will be always at your fingertips.

For more information about this title
and other APA books, visit **www.apa.org/books**.

Mastering APA Style

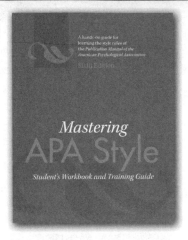

Mastering APA Style
Student's Workbook and Training Guide
SIXTH EDITION

Self-paced and self-teaching, *Mastering APA Style: Student's Workbook and Training Guide,* Sixth Edition, is an excellent way to learn official APA Style® quickly and effectively. It contains instructional exercises that teach key aspects of the *Publication Manual* to accompany the Sixth Edition, including references and citations, grammar, headings, serialization, statistical and mathematical copy, italics and capitalization, number style, and table formatting. This workbook is an effective learning module for the classroom or independent study.

2010. 228 pages. Lay-Flat Spiral Binding. ISBN 0-978-4338-0557-8.

For complete information on this and other APA books, visit **www.apa.org/books**.

Mastering APA Style

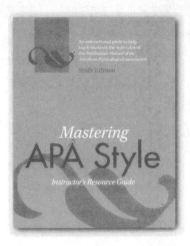

Mastering APA Style
Instructor's Resource Guide
SIXTH EDITION

Updated to accompany the Sixth Edition of the *Publication Manual*, this useful book contains suggestions on how to best utilize the *Student's Workbook and Training Guide* and offers multiple-choice assessments, answer sheets, and correction keys, along with informative instructions on how to incorporate this material into a curriculum. This guide is an effective learning tool for instructors and students to use in the classroom or as guided or independent study.

2010. 222 pages. Lay-Flat Spiral Binding. ISBN 0-978-4338-0558-5.

For complete information on this and other APA books, visit **www.apa.org/books**.